ReaL Book

SEGMENTS 1–6 | Code One

Printed in the U.S.A.

ISBN   978-0-358-73928-9

1 2 3 4 5 6 7 8 9 10   0607   31 30 29 28 27 26 25 24 23 22

4500855782   r9.22

Table of Contents

Welcome to the *ReaL Book: Code 1*

"Reading is boring." "I don't like reading." Chances are, you may have felt this way before. Reading might seem like a code that can't be cracked. And that's OK!

With some practice, YOU can crack the code.

Reading is a system made up of 26 letters and 44 sounds. Think of reading skills like the puzzle below. Most words are formed by connecting at least two pieces together. The more pieces you connect, the more words you will be able to read *and* understand.

Short Vowels You make a **short vowel** sound with the back of your throat, without slowing airflow from your mouth.

Blends Sometimes, you say two consonant sounds together and hear both sounds. That is a **blend**.

Vowel Teams A **vowel team** is made up of two vowel letters that stand for one vowel sound.

Word Parts When a **word part** is added to the beginning or end of a word, its meaning changes.

Syllable Types A **syllable** is a unit of a word with one vowel sound. Longer words usually have multiple syllables.

"Don't give up. You might be struggling, but you will end up smarter than you ever thought you could be."

Consonants You might know there are 26 letters in the alphabet. **Consonants** are letters whose sounds are formed by slowing airflow with your mouth.

VCe When you say the name of the vowel in a word, it is a long vowel sound. Words that end in a *vowel-consonant-e* pattern usually have this sound.

Digraphs Other times, you say two letters together, and they stand for one new sound. That is a **digraph**.

R-Controlled Vowels Placing an *r* after a vowel often creates a vowel sound that is neither long nor short. These are *r*-controlled vowels.

Spelling Rules Sometimes, adding a word part might change the way a word is spelled. Spelling rules explain when and why this happens.

MEET CODE BREAKER
Jamaica Williams

Jamaica Williams used to struggle in school. When she started fourth grade, she could barely read or write. She was frustrated.

Jamaica was placed in a *Read 180* classroom. It was hard, but Jamaica kept trying. The program helped her understand what she read. In time, she had the highest reading score in the class! She had finally cracked the code.

Now, Jamaica hopes to be a teacher herself.

Explore the Knowledge Map

Civil wars that split neighbors apart. People who risked their lives to do the right thing. Competitors who gave their best when it counted most. Find the topics you love and explore new worlds through Segment texts, videos, and independent reading. Use this map as a guide on your journey through content areas.

Speak Out!
Social Change | Social Studies

They risked their lives to make good things happen.

| ReaL Book: Code 1 **Making a Change** | Student App • Raise Your Voice • Harvest Hero *+ 3 more* | Independent Reading • *Poster Power* • *The Promise* *+ 9 more* |

Earth Matters
Environment | Earth Science

It's our planet. How do we keep it healthy?

| ReaL Book: Code 2 **Vines Alive!** | Student App • Trash to Treasures • Space Waste | Independent Reading • *Planting Seeds* • *Rhinos Get a Lift!* *+ 4 more* |

Showtime
Performing Arts/Literature | Literature & Fine Arts

Sometimes the struggles of life produce great art and literature.

| ReaL Book: Code 4 **Artist Diego Rivera** | Student App • A Way With Words • Art Anywhere | Independent Reading • *Fashion Flashback* • *Music Mash-Up* *+ 6 more* |

Uncivil Wars
War and Conflict | US & World History

In these conflicts it was neighbor against neighbor.

| Student App • Faked • Raise Your Voice | Independent Reading • *Home From War* • *Samurai Fighters* *+ 16 more* |

Blood, Bones, and Brains
Human Anatomy | Life Science

Uncover the mysteries of the body and the mind.

| ReaL Book: Code 3 **Sleepy Teens** | Student App • Lucky Breaks • Super Sniffers *+ 2 more* | Independent Reading • *Gross Bugs!* • *Fun Body Facts* *+22 more* |

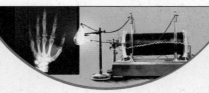

Play On!
Sports in Society | Life & Culture

Sometimes sports are more than just a game.

| ReaL Book: Code 2 **BMX Bikes Race Fast!** | Student App • Fair Play • The Robles' Roll *+ 2 more* | Independent Reading • *Sports Bloopers* • *Great Wall of Lucy Wu* *+ 10 more* |

Cluster Key—Look for these icons to find your favorite topics.

 Speak Out!　　 Earth Matters　　 Showtime　　 Uncivil Wars　　 Blood, Bones, and Brains　　Play On!

 Freedom Road　　 Moving Day　　 In Search of Hidden Worlds　　 Get Technical　　 What's Your POV?　　 True Grit

---

Freedom Road

Democracy and Civics | Social Studies

Some people brave a long journey to the land of opportunity.

Student App	Independent Reading
• Saddle Up in the City • Raise Your Voice	• *Narrative of the Life of Frederick Douglass* • *Behind Rebel Lines*

Moving Day

Immigration | Social Studies

These people have experiences in two very different worlds.

ReaL Book: Code 3 **Quiet as They Come**	Independent Reading
	• *Ballerina Dreams* • *Esperanza Rising* + 14 more

In Search of Hidden Worlds

Ancient Civilizations | World Cultures

Scientists discover the secrets of ancient civilizations.

Student App	Independent Reading
• The Hottest Job • Out of This World	• *The Mummy King* • *Ancient Army* + 16

Get Technical

Engineering | STEM

We build machines to make a better world.

ReaL Book: Code 4 **Within Her Reach**	Student App	Independent Reading
	• Space Waste • Lucky Breaks + 3 more	• *Plugged In* • *Weird Science Jobs* + 9 more

---

What's Your POV?

Argument and Debate | Life & Culture

There are at least two sides to most issues.

Student App	Independent Reading
• Out of This World • Raise Your Voice	• *Is This Art?* • *Hard Knocks* + 5 more

---

True Grit

Growth Mindset | Life & Culture

Keep your eyes on the prize and anything is possible.

ReaL Book: Code 2 **The Skywalkers' Challenge**	Student App	Independent Reading
	• The Robles' Roll • Harvest Hero + 3 more	• *Shamila's Goal* • *Everyday Heroes* + 26 more

For Stages A and C Knowledge Maps, please visit the "Resources" section on Ed.

Six Syllable Types

A syllable is a word part that has one vowel sound.

1 | Closed Syllable

A closed syllable ends in a consonant. It usually has a short vowel sound.

    a. h<u>u</u>n • dred
    b. f<u>a</u>n • tas • tic
    c. tr<u>a</u>f • fic

2 | Consonant + *-le*, *-el*, or *-al*

The consonant + *-le*, *-el*, or *-al* pattern usually forms its own syllable. You can split a word with the consonant + *-le*, *-el*, or *-al* pattern before the consonant to make it easier to read.

    a. an • <u>gle</u>
    b. tun • <u>nel</u>
    c. sig • <u>nal</u>

3 | VCe Syllable

Syllables with the vowel-consonant-*e* pattern (VCe) have a long vowel sound. When you split a word with this pattern into syllables, keep the letters of the VCe pattern together.

    a. on • <u>line</u>
    b. com • p<u>ute</u>
    c. b<u>ase</u> • ment

4 | Open Syllable

An open syllable ends in a vowel. It usually has a long vowel sound.

    a. c<u>a</u> • ble
    b. l<u>e</u> • gal
    c. m<u>u</u> • sic

5 | Vowel Team Syllable

When you split a word with a vowel team, keep the letters of the vowel team in the same syllable.

    a. con • t<u>ai</u>n
    b. r<u>ea</u> • son
    c. dis • c<u>ou</u>nt
    d. fr<u>ee</u> • dom

6 | *r*-Controlled Vowel Syllable

When the letter *r* follows a vowel, the *r* can change the sound the vowel stands for.

    a. a • p<u>ar</u>t • ment
    b. p<u>er</u> • son
    c. re • t<u>ur</u>n
    d. th<u>ir</u>st • y

Word Attack Strategy

Look ··········   Spot ··········   Split ··········   Read

Strategy	Examples	
Look for any prefixes, suffixes, or endings you know. • Remember, the spelling of the base word may have changed when the ending or suffix was added.	admitted admi<u>t</u>(t) • <u>ed</u>	undefeated <u>un</u> • defeat • <u>ed</u>
Spot the vowels in the base word. The number of vowel spots tells the number of syllables. • Remember, some vowel sounds are spelled with more than one letter.	**a**dmi**t**(t) • <u>ed</u>	un • def**ea**t • ed
Split the word into syllables. • A good place to split a word is between two consonants. • If there is only one consonant between syllables, try splitting after it. • If the word doesn't sound right, try moving the split backward or forward by one letter.	a<u>d</u> • <u>m</u>it(t) • ed	~~un • def • eat • ed~~ un • d<u>e</u> • f<u>ea</u>t • ed
Read the word. Does it make a real word? If it does not, try again. • You may need to experiment with pronouncing the vowel sound differently.	admitted	undefeated

Affixes

Prefix

A prefix is a word part added at the beginning of a base word to change its meaning.

Prefix	Meaning	Example
un-	not or opposite of	unlock
non-	not or opposite of	nonslip
de-	opposite of	defrost
com-	with	combine
con-	with	consist
re-	again	rewrite
pre-	before	pretest
mid-	in the middle of	midtown
sub-	below	subset
dis-	not or do the opposite of	disagree
mis-	badly or incorrectly	misspell
uni-	one	unicycle
bi-	two	bicycle
tri-	three	tricycle

Suffix

A suffix is a word part added at the end of a base word to change its meaning or part of speech.

Suffix	Meaning	Example
-ment	state or condition	contentment
-ness	state or condition	stillness
-y	being, having, able to	lucky
-ly	like or in a way	safely
-er	one who does something	teacher
-or	one who does something	actor
-er	compares two things or people	quicker
-est	compares more than two things or people	quickest
-less	without	spotless
-ful	causing or full of	cheerful
-tion	the state of	celebration
-sion	the state of	decision
-able	is or can be	adorable
-ible	is or can be	reversible

Roots

A root is part of an English word that comes from another language such as Latin or Greek.

Root	Meaning	Example
bio	life	*biography*
graph	something written or drawn	*graphics*
auto	self	*autobiography*
port	carry	*portable*
dict	to say	*dictate*
rupt	break	*erupts*
struct	build	*construct*
scrib/script	write	*scribble*
scope	to watch or look at	*microscope*
tele	far off	*television*
phon	sound or voice	*telephone*
vis/vid	to see	*visible*

Segment 1

Welcome to Segment 1!

Here, you'll learn about consonants, such as *m* and *s*, and the short vowel *a*. You'll also learn a word part: the ending *-s*. Together, these skills will make you a better reader. In fact, you'll use them to read a story about the unusual ways some animals sleep. So, let's get started!

Consonants
- *m, s*
- *t, n*
- *p, c*
- *b, r*

Short Vowels
- Short *a*

Word Parts
- Ending *-s*

Did you know koalas sleep up to 18 hours a day? These animals are extra tired because they eat a low-nutrient diet.

Understanding the System

The **System** is the way letters stand for sounds. There are 26 letters in the alphabet. These letters spell the 44 most common sounds in English.

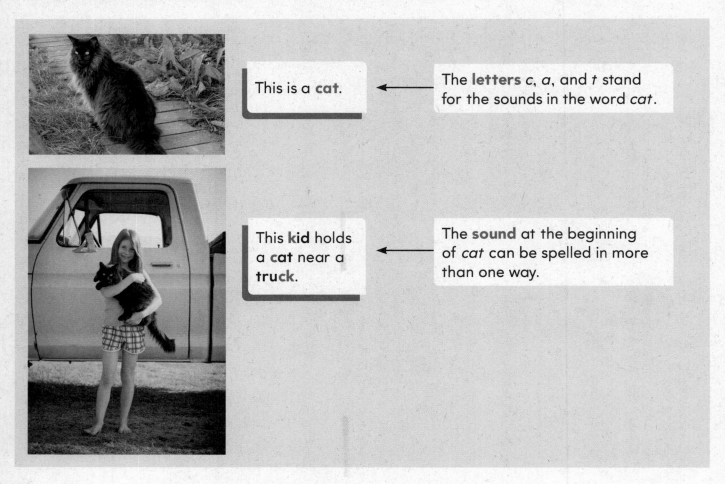

This is a **cat**.

The **letters** c, a, and t stand for the sounds in the word *cat*.

This **kid** holds a **cat** near a **truck**.

The **sound** at the beginning of *cat* can be spelled in more than one way.

Find It

Look at the "Consonants" section of the System of Sounds and Spellings poster. Find a word that matches each underlined consonant below. Copy the word into the space next to it. Circle the beginning letter.

1. <u>c</u>ut _____
2. <u>s</u>et _____
3. <u>b</u>eg _____

4. <u>l</u>et _____
5. <u>f</u>it _____
6. <u>d</u>id _____

7. <u>v</u>et _____
8. <u>h</u>ot _____
9. <u>r</u>ug _____

Keyword Match

Say the name of each picture. Find the picture on the poster. How many ways are there to spell the sound?

1.  book _____

2.  cat _____

3.  chair _____

4.  email _____

5.  ship _____

6.  fan _____

7.  chop _____

8.  table _____

9.  sun _____

10.  infant _____

Identifying & Understanding Consonants & Vowels

Words are made up of **consonants** and **vowels**. Every word has at least one vowel sound. The vowel letters are *a, e, i, o, u,* and sometimes *y*.

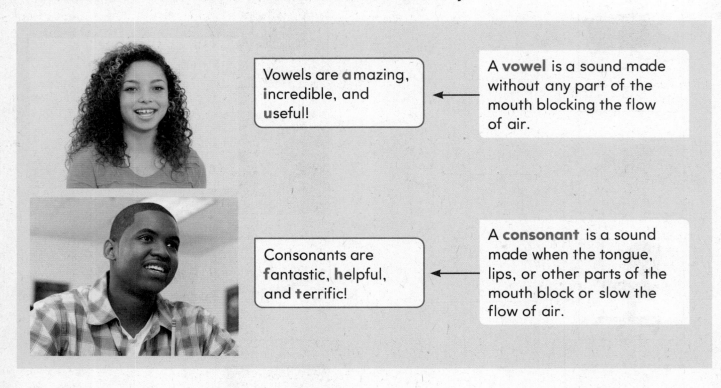

Vowels are **a**mazing, **i**ncredible, and **u**seful!

A **vowel** is a sound made without any part of the mouth blocking the flow of air.

Consonants are **f**antastic, **h**elpful, and **t**errific!

A **consonant** is a sound made when the tongue, lips, or other parts of the mouth block or slow the flow of air.

Find It

Circle the vowels. Underline the consonants.

1. c u t
2. a c t
3. q u i c k
4. p a r t

5. f i n
6. t r i p
7. e a t
8. a p e

9. a x
10. h i m
11. v a n
12. h i l l

Word List

Name the first letter in each word. Then, underline it. The first one is started for you.

a̲dd	cap	ox	fit	den	van
bun	us	end	ink	rub	act

Sort It

Write each word from above in the correct box.

Begins With a Vowel	Begins With a Consonant
add	cap

Write It

PART A Write an *m* under the pictures whose names begin with *m*.

1.

_____   _____   _____

2.

_____   _____   _____

PART B Write an *s* under the pictures whose names begin with *s*.

3.

_____   _____   _____

4.

_____   _____   _____

REVIEW

- Consonant *m* stands for the sound you hear at the beginning of the word *map* and at the end of the word *jam*.

- Consonant *s* stands for the sound you hear at the beginning of the word *sun*.

Vocabulary Builder

Read each word, its part of speech, and its meaning.

Then write a sentence using the word.

Target Word Read the target words.	Meaning Think about the meanings.	Example Complete each sentence using the target word.
mad (adjective)	very angry	I feel _____ when _____ _____ _____
map (noun)	a plan of a place	I look at a _____ when _____ _____
met (verb)	came face to face with someone	I have _____ someone at ___ _____ _____
sad (adjective)	unhappy	A _____ movie I have seen is _____ _____
sun (noun)	the star that gives us light and warmth	I can see the_____ _____ _____

Comic

Sam

I **am** Sam!

Am I Sam?

I **am!**

Choose the Correct Answer

1. Who sees Sam?

    a. A cat sees Sam.

    b. Sam sees Sam.

    c. A man sees Sam.

2. How does Sam feel in the second picture?

    a. surprised

    b. angry

    c. happy

Text Message

Word Count: 6

Text Message

Are you OK?

I am OK.

I am 2!

Choose the Correct Answer

1. Is everyone OK?

    a. yes

    b. no

Comic

Sssssnake!

Choose the Correct Answer

1. Who is scared?

   a. the snake

   b. the man

   c. both

2. What sound does the snake make?

   a. Sssssssss!

   b. Aaaaaaaa!!!

Comic

Stan's Bad Day

Choose the Correct Answer

1. What problem is Stan having?

    a. He is sweating.

    b. He has a flat tire.

    c. It is raining.

2. Look at the picture. What does Stan mean when he says, "Mmmmmmm!"?

    a. Stan is eating something delicious.

    b. Stan feels mad.

Write It

PART A Write a *t* under the pictures whose names begin with *t*.

1.
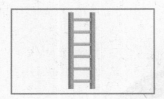

2.

PART B Write an *n* under the pictures whose names begin with *n*.

3.

4.

Vocabulary Builder

Read each word, its part of speech, and its meaning.

Then write a sentence using the word.

Target Word Read the target words.	Meaning Think about the meanings.	Example Complete each sentence using the target word.
hot (adjective)	high in temperature	Something that is _____ is a _____ _____
men (noun)	adult males	Two teachers who are_____ are _____.____ _____
nose (noun)	the part of your face you use to smell	Something I like to smell with my _____ is _____ _____
pet (noun)	a tame animal	My favorite kind of_____ is a _____ _____
tiger (noun)	a big, striped, wild cat found in Asia	I could see a _____ _____ _____

Comic

Word Count: 2

Get Up, Nat!

Match It

Draw a line from each question to its correct answer.

1. What object is behind the woman?

    in bed

2. What is the woman pointing to?

    a coffee maker

3. How does the woman feel?

    hiding under the covers

4. Where is Nat?

    annoyed

5. What is Nat doing?

    her watch

Comic

Word Count: 9

Stan's Day

Stan **sat at** 5 A.M.

Stan **sat at** 9 A.M.

Stan **sat at** 8 P.M.

Choose the Correct Answer

1. What does Stan do first?

   a. work at a desk

   b. read a newspaper

   c. see a movie

2. What does Stan do next?

   a. ride on a train

   b. see a movie

   c. work at a desk

3. What does Stan do last?

   a. spill popcorn

   b. work at a desk

   c. ride on a train

Comic

Word Count: 5

Nan Tricks Ann (Part 1)

Choose the Correct Answer

1. What happens in the first picture?

   a. Ann texts.

   b. Matt texts.

2. What time does Matt want to meet Ann?

   a. 6:00

   b. 7:00

   c. 8:00

Comic

Nan Tricks Ann (Part 2)

At 8:00 P.M.

Choose the Correct Answer

1. Who is wearing pajamas?

    a. Ann

    b. Nan

    c. Matt

2. Review Parts 1 and 2 of the story. Why isn't Ann ready for the date?

    a. She forgot about the date.

    b. She never saw the message about the date.

    c. She does not like flowers.

Contrasting Long & Short Vowels

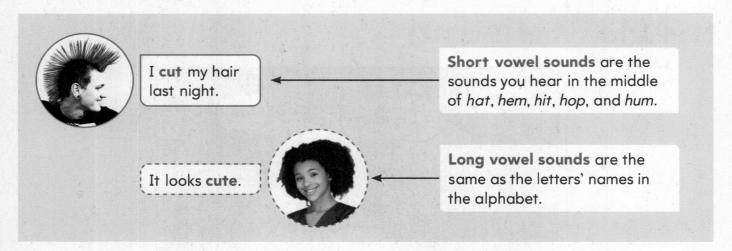

I **cut** my hair last night.

It looks **cute**.

Short vowel sounds are the sounds you hear in the middle of *hat*, *hem*, *hit*, *hop*, and *hum*.

Long vowel sounds are the same as the letters' names in the alphabet.

Long Vowel Sounds

Write the letter of the long vowel sound you hear read aloud.

1. s ☐ m e   4. h ☐ m e
2. ☐ v e   5. m ☐ t e
3. m ☐ n e   6. ☐ t e

Short Vowel Sounds

Write the letter of the short vowel sound you hear read aloud.

7. b ☐ t   10. l ☐ t
8. l ☐ d   11. r ☐ n
9. h ☐ t   12. ☐ t

Long and Short Vowel Sounds

Circle the words with short vowel sounds. Underline the words with long vowel sounds.

hid	hide	cod	code
huge	hug	mad	made

Practice

Write the short and long vowel words in the correct boxes.

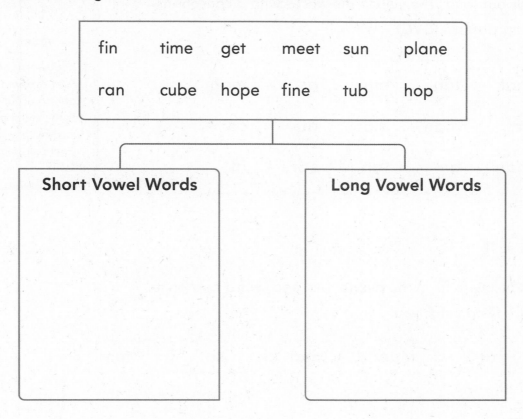

fin   time   get   meet   sun   plane

ran   cube   hope   fine   tub   hop

Short Vowel Words

Long Vowel Words

Context Clues

Write the correct word in the blank.

1. I _____ an apple. (at, ate)

2. I stayed _____ my cousin's house. (at, ate)

3. I had a _____ in my jeans. (rip, ripe)

4. The fruit was _____. (rip, ripe)

5. I took a bath in the _____. (tub, tube)

6. Air moved through the _____. (tub, tube)

Apply the Code

Word List

Read the words out loud. Then circle the words with a consonant-vowel-consonant pattern (CVC).

sat	mat	tan	am	an	man
at	sat	man	mat	at	sat
am	man	an	tan	sat	at

REVIEW

m<u>a</u>n • t<u>a</u>n

These words have the **short a vowel sound.** Letter **a** usually stands for the **short a** sound in words with a consonant-vowel-consonant pattern (CVC).

Puzzle Fun

Use the words below to fill in the puzzle. Use each word only once. Some letters are filled in for you.

an	at	man	mat	sat	tan

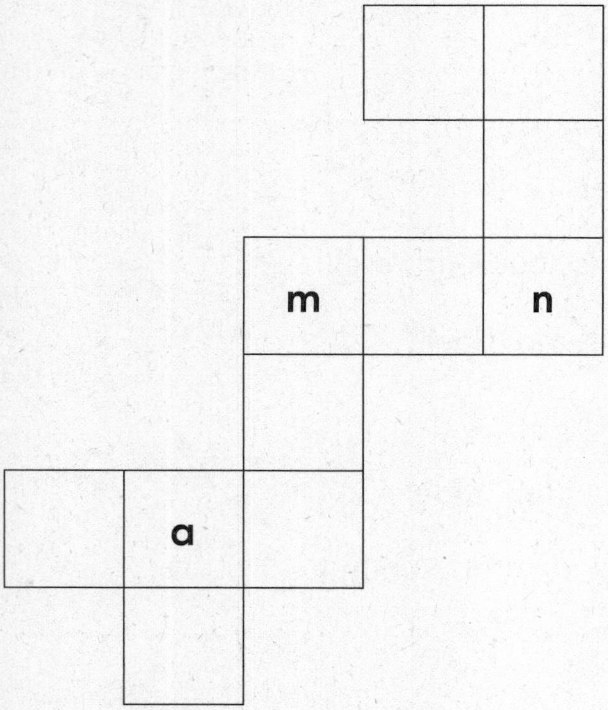

(puzzle grid with letters m, n, a)

Vocabulary Builder

Read each word, its part of speech, and its meaning.

Then write a sentence using the word.

Target Word Read the target words.	Meaning Think about the meanings.	Example Complete each sentence using the target word.
am (verb)	the form of the verb *to be* that is used with *I*	Today, I _____ _____ _____
at (preposition)	in a particular place	_____ a grocery store, I can buy _____ _____
man (noun)	an adult male person	The _____ was at the bank to _____ _____
mat (noun)	a piece of thick material that covers part of a floor	I can use a _____ to _____ _____ _____
tan (adjective)	a light, yellow-brown color	I have a _____ _____ _____

Ant and Man?

A tan mat An ant A man A man! An ant! A tan mat!

Choose the Correct Answer

1. Who sat?

 a. the ant

 b. the man

 c. the ant and the man

2. Who looked upset, the ant or the man?

 a. the ant

 b. the man

3. Where did the ant sit?

 a. on the tan mat

 b. on the man

Comic

A Man

A man sat.

A **man sat.**

A **man sat**
and **sat.**

A **man sat.**

Choose the Correct Answer

1. What did the man sit down to do?

   a. He sat to read.

   b. He sat to eat.

2. What happened to the man?

   a. He got up.

   b. He fell asleep.

Blending Sounds Into Words

These letters make the sounds /g/, /e/, and /t/. Blended together, that's **get**.

Oh, I get it!

g e t

Words are made up of individual **sounds**.

The single sounds are blended together to make a word.

Blend It

Listen to the sound each letter stands for. Then blend the sounds together to make a word. Write the word on the line.

1. m a n
_____

2. g o t
_____

3. n o d
_____

4. th e n
_____

5. n e s t
_____

6. t u s k
_____

7. s t o ck
_____

8. s p i ll
_____

9. b l e n d
_____

Picture Perfect

Listen to the sounds in each word. Blend the sounds together.
Then write the word beside its picture below.

1. sob

2. sun

3. jet

4. pin

5. neck

6. map

 _____

 _____

 _____

_____

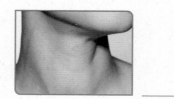 _____

_____

Sentence Solver

Choose the correct words to complete the sentences.

1. We _____ use this _____ to cool the room. (fan, can)

2. It is too _____ to wear this _____ (hot, hat)

3. Please bring _____ my _____ (back, bag)

4. We _____ down the hill on a _____ (sled, slid)

Segmenting Words Into Sounds

How do you spell your name?

Segment, or break, a word into its sounds.

Blend the sounds together to read the word.

It's J-O-N. Jon.

Count It

Read each word. Count the number of sounds in each word. Write the number on the line.

1. am _____   3. it _____   5. yes _____

2. hat _____   4. trim _____   6. back _____

Segment It

Break each word into its sounds. Write each sound in a box.

1. an ☐☐   4. went ☐☐☐☐

2. sun ☐☐☐   5. if ☐☐

3. pot ☐☐☐   6. mop ☐☐☐

Sort It

Write the words with two sounds and the words with three sounds in the correct boxes.

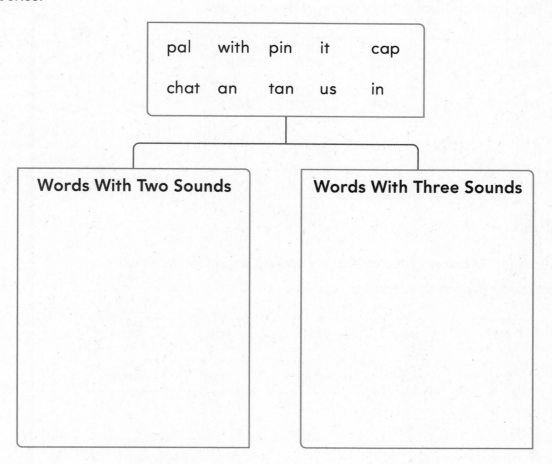

| pal | with | pin | it | cap |
| chat | an | tan | us | in |

Words With Two Sounds

Words With Three Sounds

Segment and Spell

Write the letters of the words you hear read aloud.

1. _____ _____

2. _____ _____ _____

3. _____ _____ _____

4. _____ _____ _____

5. _____ _____ _____

Word List

Read the words out loud. Then circle the words that begin with **p** as in **_pan_**. Underline the words that begin with **c** as in **_cat_**.

can	cap	an	tap	pan	sap
mat	at	cat	sat	man	pat
an	can	tap	at	pat	pan

REVIEW

pan • cat

- Consonant **p** stands for the sound you hear at the beginning of the word **pan**.
- Consonant **c** can stand for the sound you hear at the beginning of the word **cat**.

Rhyme It

Read the words in the boxes. Then find four rhyming words for each word listed below. The first one is started for you.

map	cat	pan	nap	tan	mat
pat	tap	sat	sap	can	man

1. an ___pan___ ___tan___ _____ _____

2. at _____ _____ _____ _____

3. cap _____ _____ _____ _____

Vocabulary Builder

Read each word, its part of speech, and its meaning.

Then write a sentence using the word.

Target Word Read the target words.	Meaning Think about the meanings.	Example Complete each sentence using the target word.
can (verb)	to be able to do something	I _____ play _____ _____ _____
cap (noun)	a soft hat with a peak at the front	I wear a _____ at _____ _____ _____
cat (noun)	a small animal with fur and claws, often kept as a pet	I would give a _____ the name _____ _____
map (noun)	a drawing of an area	I would use a _____ to _____ _____ _____
pan (noun)	a round metal pot used for cooking	I would use a _____ to _____ _____ _____

Comic

Word Count: 21

Sap on a Cap

A tan **cap**

A **pan** of **sap**

A tan **cap!**
A **pan** of **sap!**

A tan **cap!**
A **tap!** A **tap!**

Match It

Draw a line from each question to its correct answer.

1. What is the man doing in the first picture?   washing with water from a tap

2. What is happening to the tan
   cap in the third picture?   walking and whistling

3. What saves the tan cap?   flying into some sap

Order the Events

Put the events of the story in the order in which they happen.

4. Number each sentence 1, 2, or 3.

   _____ A man washes his hat with water.

   _____ A man in a tan cap walks in the woods.

   _____ A tan cap lands in some sap.

Comic

Word Count: 21

A Map Nap?

Nan **pats** Sam, a tan cat.

Nan sat at a **map.**

Sam naps.

Nan **taps** Sam. "Sam, my **map!**"

Choose the Correct Answer

1. What color is Nan's cat?

   a. tan

   b. pink

   c. black

2. Who naps on a map?

   a. the cat

   b. Nan

   c. the rat

3. Why does Nan want the cat to move?

   a. She wants to pat the cat.

   b. She can't see the map.

   c. The cat is tan.

Comic

Cat Spat

Pat, a **cat**, naps on a mat.

Sam, a tan **cat**, taps Pat.

Sam, **can** Pat nap?

Choose the Correct Answer

1. Who naps on the mat?

   a. Pat

   b. Sam

2. Who is the tan cat?

   a. Pat

   b. Sam

3. Who wants to nap?

   a. Pat

   b. Sam

Postcard

Word Count: 28

At Camp Sacnac

Ann,

I am at **Camp** Sacnac!

I got tan at **Camp.**

Can you send a **cap**
and some pants?

Love,

Cam

Ann Capp
5 Pappas Ct.
Canton, CT 06109

Forever
USA

Choose the Correct Answer

1. What happened to Cam at Camp Sacnac?

    a. She got tan.

    b. She tore her pants.

2. What does she need?

    a. a map

    b. some pants

3. Who does Cam write to?

    a. Dan

    b. Ann

Word List

Read the words out loud. Then circle the words that begin with **b** as in <u>**b**at</u>. Underline the words that begin with **r** as in <u>**r**an</u>.

bat	rat	cab	rap	cap	ban
can	tan	ran	sat	ram	pat
rap	cab	bat	ban	tan	can

Write It

Read the words in the boxes. Then write the correct word next to each picture.

bat	can	cab	cat	pan	map

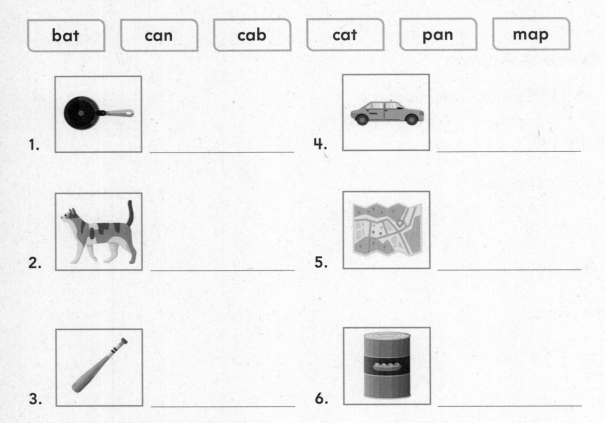

1. _____

2. _____

3. _____

4. _____

5. _____

6. _____

Vocabulary Builder

Read each word, its part of speech, and its meaning.

Then write a sentence using the word.

Target Word Read the target words.	Meaning Think about the meanings.	Example Complete each sentence using the target word.
ban (verb)	to forbid something	Movie theaters can _____ people from _____ _____
bat (noun)	a long piece of wood used for hitting a baseball	I can buy a _____ at the ____ _____ _____
ram (noun)	a male sheep	A _____ has _____ _____ _____ on his head.
ran (verb)	to have moved very quickly, using the legs	When I _____ , I _____ _____ _____
rap (noun)	a kind of music with words that are spoken in time with the music	My favorite _____ is _____ _____ _____

Word Count: 15

Comic

Nat and a Cab

Nat ran at a **cab**.
Nat sat.

Bam! Bam! Bam!

Nat sat on a **cab**!

Write It

Write a full sentence to answer the question.

1. What is a cab?

Choose the Correct Answer

2. What happened first?

   a. Nat sat on a cab.

   b. Bam! Bam! Bam!

3. Why did Nat sit on a cab?

   a. The cab had no gas.

   b. The cab had a flat.

   c. Nat was late.

Brant at Bat

Brant is at **bat.** Brant is at a mat. Brant pats a cap. Brant taps a **bat.** Brant taps a mat. Brant can **bat!**

Match It

Draw a line from each question to its correct answer.

1. What is Brant playing?   at a mat

2. Who can bat?   Brant

3. Where is Brant?   baseball

Fiction

Word Count: 17

Pam, a Cat, a Rat, and a Bat

A cat can 👁 a **rat**.

A **rat** can 👁 Pam.

Pam can 👁 a bat.

Can a bat 👁 them?

Match It

Draw a line from each question to its correct answer.

1. Who can see Pam?

2. Who can see the rat?

3. Who can Pam see?

a cat

a rat

a bat

Comic

No Rest for a Rat

A **rat** naps.

A cat! A **rat**!

A **rat** can't nap.

Choose the Correct Answer

1. What happens in the beginning of the story?

    a. A rat naps.

    b. A rat pats a cat.

2. Why can't the rat nap?

    a. The rat can't nap because of the cat.

    b. The rat can't nap because of the bat.

Word List

Read the words out loud. Then circle the words with an **-s ending.**

cans	map	raps	pat	pans	mats
tab	pats	cabs	rams	nap	can
bats	naps	bat	caps	cat	cap

Sentence Solver

Use a word from the word bank to complete each sentence.

naps   bats   cats

1. He pats the _____ .
2. Pam _____ .
3. Cam _____ .

Mark It

Underline each base word and circle each word ending.
The first one is done for you.

4. <u>pat</u>(s)

5. naps

6. bats

Vocabulary Builder

Read each word, its part of speech, and its meaning.

Then write a sentence using the word.

Target Word Read the target words.	Meaning Think about the meanings.	Example Complete each sentence using the target word.
naps (noun)	short periods of sleep	I like to take _____ at_____ _____ _____
caps (noun)	small hats	My favorite team wears _____ that are _____ _____
cabs (noun)	cars that take people places for a fee	I see _____ at_____ _____ _____
bats (noun)	small, furry animals that fly mostly at night	_____ live _____ _____ _____
cats (noun)	furry animals with claws, pointy ears, and long tails	As pets, I think _____ are _____ _____

Poem

Word Count: 12

A Band Jams

Sam **taps cans.**

Nat **taps pans.**

Pat **snaps.**

Tad **raps.**

A band!

Choose the Correct Answer

1. How many people are in the band?

   a. two

   b. three

   c. four

2. Who taps cans?

   a. Tad

   b. Sam

   c. Nat

3. Who snaps?

   a. Pat

   b. Sam

   c. Nat

Comic

Word Count: 11

Sam's Maps

Maps

Sam **scans maps.**

Sam **stamps maps.**

Sam **camps** with **maps.**

Write It

Write a sentence to answer the question.

1. What are two things Sam does with maps?

_____

_____

_____

Choose the Correct Answer

2. What does Sam carry with her when she camps?

    a. sunglasses

    b. a backpack

    c. an umbrella

Recognizing & Using Possessives

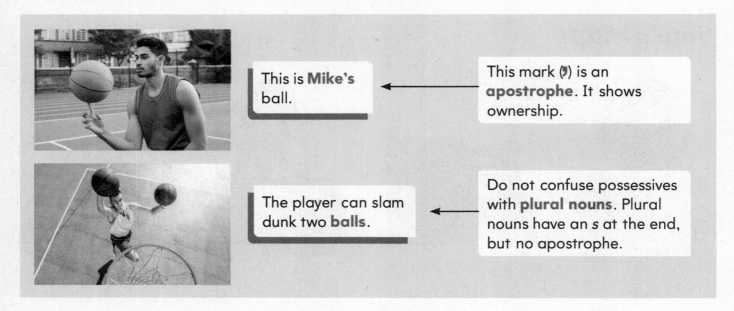

This is **Mike's** ball.

This mark (') is an **apostrophe**. It shows ownership.

The player can slam dunk two **balls**.

Do not confuse possessives with **plural nouns**. Plural nouns have an *s* at the end, but no apostrophe.

Write Possessives

Rewrite each sentence using a possessive noun.

1. The fur of the cat is black. _The cat's fur is black._____

2. The cover of the book is red. _____

3. The bowl of the dog is empty. _____

4. The home of Kim is huge. _____

5. The pants of the man are red. _____

6. These are the bikes of Jose. _____

Contrast Singular and Plural Possessives

If a noun is **plural**, the possessive ends with an apostrophe after the letter *s*.

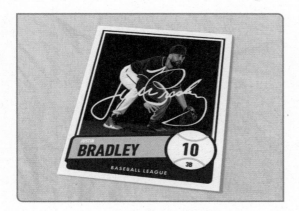

one baseball **player's** autograph

many baseball **players'** autographs

Practice

Circle the singular possessive nouns. Underline the plural possessive nouns.

cat's collar   maps   dogs' bowls   students' pens

fans' cheers   pin's message   lines   home's door

Revise Sentences

Rewrite each sentence using a singular or plural possessive noun.

1. These are the hats of the team. These are the team's hats. _____

2. The shirt of my sister is green. _____

3. This is the food of the birds. _____

4. The sons of Brad are tall. _____

5. The horns of the cars are loud. _____

6. The room of my brothers is big. _____

Segment 2

Welcome to Segment 2!

In Segment 2, you'll learn the short vowels *i* and *o*. Moving on, you'll study new consonants, such as *d* and *f*. You'll also learn about the digraph *-ck*. These skills will help you read an awesome story about a popular dance—breaking. Ready? Let's go!

Short Vowels

- Short *i*
- Short *o*

Consonants

- *d, f*
- *h, k*
- *l, x*

Digraphs

- *-ck*

Most breakdancers have great athletic abilities. One dancer in Japan actually performed 139 nonstop one-hand jumps, like the one shown here!

Word List

Read the words out loud. Then circle the words with **short i** as in *rip*.

in	sip	it	tin	sap	bat
pin	tan	rap	sit	rim	tip
pan	bit	taps	sat	mats	rip

REVIEW

rip • pin

These words have the **short i vowel sound.** Letter *i* usually stands for the **short i** sound in words with a consonant-vowel-consonant pattern (CVC).

Sentence Solver

Use the words below to complete each sentence. Use the pictures to help you. The first one is done for you.

sip	rim	rip	sit	bit	pin

1. It hit the _____ rim _____ .

2. This has a _____ in it.

3. My cap has a _____ .

4. I _____ in the cab.

5. Tim _____ into the ribs.

6. I can _____ from the tap.

Vocabulary Builder

Read each word, its part of speech, and its meaning.

Then write a sentence using the word.

Target Word Read the target words.	Meaning Think about the meanings.	Example Complete each sentence using the target word.
bit (verb)	to have cut something with your teeth	I was hungry, so I _____ into _____ _____
pin (noun)	a short, thin piece of metal with a sharp point	I would use a _____ to _____ _____ _____
pit (noun)	a hole in the ground made by digging	Workers could dig a _____ to _____ _____
rib (noun)	one of the 12 pairs of curved bones in the chest	She injured her _____ playing _____ _____
tip (noun)	the end of something	I use the _____ of a pen for _____ _____

List

Bill's Packing List

A list

- ☑ a bat
- ☑ a **mitt**
- ☑ tan pants
- ☑ a cap
- ☑ Pam's **pic**

Choose the Correct Answer

1. Whose list is this?

    a. It is Bill's list.

    b. It is Pam's list.

2. What is Bill packing for?

    a. to play sports

    b. to learn in school

3. How many items are on the list?

    a. 5

    b. 8

Word Count: 21

Comic

Homework Fibs?

A cat sat **in it!**   I am sick **in** bed!   A man ran at **it!**   **It** has a **rip in it!**

Choose the Correct Answer

1. How did the cat ruin the homework?

    a. It sat in it.

    b. It ran with it.

2. How does the person in bed look?

    a. She looks mad.

    b. She looks sick.

3. How big is the rip on the page?

    a. It is a small rip.

    b. It is a big rip.

Word List

Read the words out loud. Then circle the words that begin with *d* as in <u>*dog*</u>. Underline the words that begin with *f* as in <u>*fan*</u>.

fan	rid	ran	fad	mad	fit
sit	fin	rim	mats	bad	sip
dim	dip	bat	in	sad	tip

All Mixed Up

Unscramble the sentences. Write them on the line.

1. bit I bad rib a _____

2. sad not Dad is _____

3. has pan lid The a _____

4. pan in fits the It _____

5. cat My fat is _____

6. tip fan The can _____

Vocabulary Builder

Read each word, its part of speech, and its meaning.

Then write a sentence using the word.

Target Word Read the target words.	Meaning Think about the meanings.	Example Complete each sentence using the target word.
bad (adjective)	not good or not nice	Foods that are _____ for me are _____ _____
dim (adjective)	not very bright	The light is _____ indoors when _____ _____
fan (noun)	an object for moving air around to cool you	I use a _____ when _____ _____ _____
fit (verb)	to be the right size or shape	Clothes might not_____ because _____ _____
mad (adjective)	very angry	The things that make me _____ are _____ _____

Fiction

Word Count: 23

Dad and Dibs

Dibs is my cat. Dibs bit Dad and ran! **Bad** cat!

Dad was **mad**. Dad ran, and so **did** Dibs, the bad cat!

Match It

Draw a line from each question to its correct answer.

1. Who is Dibs?   He ran.

2. What did Dibs do wrong?   He bit Dad.

3. What did Dad do?   He is a cat.

Write It

Write a sentence to answer the question.

4. What did Dad and Dibs both do?

_____

Word Count: 43

The Bad Rap on Bats

It is sad. A bat has a **bad, bad** rap. A bat can nap in the day. And a bat can get **rid** of **bad** pests! Is a bat **bad?**

Are you **mad** at a bat's **bad** rap? Are you a bat fan?

Choose the Correct Answer

1. What does it mean to have a bad rap?

    a. that you can't play the drums

    b. that people think bad things about you

Write It

Write a sentence to answer the question.

2. What are two things a bat can do?

_____

_____

Fiction

Word Count: 33

Fans for Sale

   "**Fan**-tastic!" has **fans**. Fran ran a bad ad for "**Fan**-tastic!" Fran's ad has a bad, bad mistake. Fran is sad, and Fran is mad! Fran has a **fit**! Is it Fran's last ad?

Choose the Correct Answer

1. What is Fan-tastic?

    a. Fan-tastic is a restaurant.

    b. Fan-tastic is a store.

    c. Fan-tastic is a person.

2. What does Fan-tastic sell?

    a. ads

    b. food

    c. fans

3. How does Fran feel about the ad?

    a. happy

    b. sick

    c. mad

Fiction

Word Count: 21

Fast Fins

Tim straps on **fins**.

He dips in!

He taps a crab.

The crab is mad!

Tim can swim **fast**!

Scram, crab!

Match It

Draw a line from each question to its correct answer.

1. What does Tim strap on his feet?

2. What sport does Tim do?

3. What does Tim tell the crab to do?

swim

scram

fins

Word List

Read the words out loud. Then circle the words that begin with *h* as in <u>*hat*</u>. Underline the words that begin with *k* as in <u>*kid*</u>.

dim	had	hip	tip	can	hid
hat	fin	ram	him	bad	kin
rid	kit	maps	kid	hit	cabs

REVIEW

<u>hat</u> • <u>kid</u>

- Consonant *h* stands for the sound you hear at the beginning of the word *hat*.
- Consonant *k* stands for the sound you hear at the beginning of the word *kid*.

Math Facts

Change the letters to spell new words. Then write the words on the lines to make a sentence. The first one has been done for you.

1. bid – b + h = <u>hid</u>   ham – m + t = <u>hat</u>

   Kit <u>hid</u> my <u>hat</u> .

2. pad – p + h = _____   hat – h + f = _____   fat – f + c = _____

   Kim _____ a _____ _____ .

3. mat – t + n = _____   tap – p + n = _____   can – n + p = _____

   The _____ has a _____ _____ .

4. in – n + s = _____   hit – i + a = _____

   This _____ my _____ .

5. kit – t + d = _____   mat – t + p = _____

   This _____ has a _____ .

Vocabulary Builder

Read each word, its part of speech, and its meaning.

Then write a sentence using the word.

Target Word Read the target words.	Meaning Think about the meanings.	Example Complete each sentence using the target word.
had (verb)	possessed something	The best toy I ever_____ was _____ _____
hat (noun)	an item of clothing worn on the head	I wear a _____ when _____ _____ _____
hid (verb)	kept something from sight	I _____ my _____ _____ _____
hit (verb)	to strike something with your hand or with a tool	To _____ a ball, I can use a _____ _____
kit (noun)	a set of tools or things used for a certain purpose	One thing in a first aid _____ would be _____ _____

Fiction

Word Count: 22

Ham in a Can?

This is in Kim's bag. **Ham** in a can and mints in a tin? Can Kim skip this? It is bad!

Choose the Correct Answer

1. What is in Kim's bag?

    a. ham in a can and mints in a tin

    b. ham in a tin and mints in a can

2. What might Kim say about the things in her bag?

    a. "I am so glad!"

    b. "This is bad!"

Fiction

Word Count: 32

Frank's Big Hit

Frank is at bat. Frank **hits** the ball. Frank **hits** it fast. Frank **hits** a home run!

A fan in the stands tips his **hat.** "I am a fan! The kid is fast!"

Choose the Correct Answer

1. Read the passage. How does Frank hit the ball?

   a. Frank hits it fast.

   b. Frank hits it first.

2. What does the fan say about Frank?

   a. "The kid is fast!"

   b. "Frank is at bat!"

Comic

Word Count: 23

Kip's Kit

Kip is a **kid.** Kip has a **kit.**

Kip did his **kit.**

Is Kip's **kit** bad?

His **kit** is bad!

Order the Events

Put the events of the story in the order in which they happen.

1. Number each sentence 1, 2, or 3.

    _____ The robot comes to life.

    _____ Kip builds the robot.

    _____ Kip opens a robot kit.

Choose the Correct Answer

2. Why is Kip unhappy with his kit?

    a. He can't figure out how to build the robot.

    b. The robot comes to life and scares him.

Fiction

Word Count: 28

Kam's Pants

Kam has pants. The pants have a rip. Kam has a **kit**. The **kit** has pins. The **kit** has thread. Kam fixes the rip in his pants.

Choose the Correct Answer

1. What is the problem with Kam's pants?

    a. He can't find them.

    b. They have a rip.

2. How does Kam fix the problem with his pants?

    a. He sews them.

    b. He decides to get new pants instead.

Write It

Write a sentence to answer the question.

3. Kam's kit has pins. What else does his kit have?

_____

Apply the Code

Word List

Read the words out loud. Then put a star by the words with **short o** as in **h_o_t.**

hop	hip	sob	pop	tip	nod
cats	kit	mats	map	tap	mop
top	pit	not	dot	pat	mom

REVIEW

h_o_t • m_o_p

These words have the **short o vowel sound.** Letter *o* usually stands for the **short o** sound in words with a consonant-vowel-consonant pattern (CVC).

Puzzle Fun

Use the word bank to fill in the puzzle. One is done for you.

dot	top	stop	cob
pot	mop	sob	cot

Across

2.

5.

6.

Down

1.

2.

3.

4.

5.

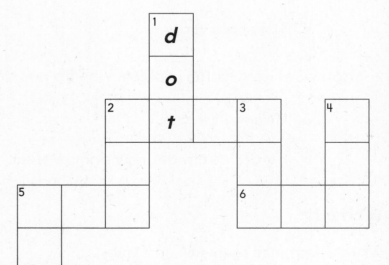

Vocabulary Builder

Read each word, its part of speech, and its meaning.

Then write a sentence using the word.

Target Word Read the target words.	Meaning Think about the meanings.	Example Complete each sentence using the target word.
hop (verb)	to move with short jumps or leaps	An animal that can _____ is _____ _____
hot (adjective)	having a high temperature	A _____ food that I like to eat is _____ _____
mom (noun)	_informal_; a word that means _mother_	A new _____ might _____ _____ _____
not (adjective)	at no time or in no way	I do _____ like _____ _____ _____
top (noun)	the highest point or part	I can climb to the _____ of _____ _____

Make Meaning

Ad

Word Count: 31

Top Mop Hits the Spot!

Got **spots?** You **cannot** miss the **spots** with this **mop!**

- ☑ An ink **dot?**
- ☑ Sand bits?
- ☑ Hand prints?

It is OK! It is **not** bad! The EZ **Mop** can **top** any **mop!**

Choose the Correct Answer

1. The EZ Mop can clean up sand bits.

    a. true

    b. false

2. The EZ Mop ad shows a picture of a clean floor.

    a. true

    b. false

78 Segment 2 • Lesson 4

Fiction

Word Count: 39

Dot and Spot

Dot is Todd's cat. Dot is **not** fit. In fact, Dot is fat. And Dot naps a lot.

Todd got Spot. Spot is fit and fast! Spot chases Dot nonstop. Dot is mad at Spot. Dot is **not** fast!

Match It

Draw a line from each question to its correct answer.

1. Who naps a lot?   Spot

2. Who is fast?   Dot

3. Who got Spot?   Todd

Choose the Correct Answer

4. Why is Dot mad at Spot?

   a. Dot does not nap.

   b. Spot is faster than Dot.

Word List

Read the words out loud. Then circle the words that begin with
l as in **li<u>ps</u>**. Underline the words that end with **x** as in **bo<u>x</u>**.

lab	mom	lit	six	sit	fix
fox	tip	box	hot	fit	tab
lot	lips	pot	lap	mix	cans

Find It

Read each clue. Write the word from the word bank that goes with
the clue. The first one is done for you.

lip	six	fin	fox
cat	pot	tan	map

1. I am 4 + 2. ___six___

2. I can help you find where you are going. _____

3. You use me to cook. _____

4. I am a part of a fish. _____

5. I am a wild animal. _____

6. I am a color. _____

Vocabulary Builder

Read each word, its part of speech, and its meaning.

Then write a sentence using the word.

Target Word Read the target words.	Meaning Think about the meanings.	Example Complete each sentence using the target word.
box (noun)	a container with four flat sides	One food that comes in a _____ is _____ _____
lid (noun)	a cover for a pot or a box	I put a _____ on _____ _____ _____
lit (verb)	started to burn something	If I _____ a campfire, I would cook _____ _____
mix (verb)	to put different things together	I _____ together_____ _____ _____
six (adjective)	having the amount of the number 6	When I was _____ years old, I lived _____ _____

Word Count: 31

Late at the Lab

Bill is at his **lab**. Bill **lifts** a kit. It tips!
Bill drops the kit. The **lid** on the kit pops!

Now Bill must stop and mop the spill.
Poor Bill!

Write It

Write a sentence to answer each question.

1. When does the lid on the kit pop?

    _____

2. What must Bill stop and do?

    _____

3. Based on what you know about Bill, what kind of job does he have?

    _____

List

Word Count: 30

Lil's List

Lil has a long list. This is Lil's list:

- ☑ ham in a tin can
- ☑ a pot and a lid
- ☑ milk
- ☑ a mop

Can Lil fit it all in a box?

Choose the Correct Answer

1. Look at the picture. What is Lil doing?

    a. shopping

    b. leaning

    c. cooking

2. What is one thing on Lil's list?

    a. a pan

    b. a mop

    c. a hat

Comic

Word Count: 41

Rod and His Sax

Rod has to **fix** his **sax** at **six**. Rod drops his **sax** in a **box** and flips the lid.

Rod runs at a cab. Rod drops his **sax**!

A cab hits it! Rod is mad!

Can he **fix** his **sax** now?

Match It

Draw a line from each question to its correct answer.

1. What hits the sax?   Rod

2. What time will Rod fix his sax?   six

3. Who drops the sax?   a cab

Order the Events

Put the events of the story in the order in which they happen.

4. Number each sentence 1, 2, or 3.

_____ Rod gets mad.   _____ Rod drops his sax in a box.   _____ A cab hits the sax.

Fiction

Word Count: 28

Ann and Max

Ann and Max are in the lab. Max has a hot pan. Ann adds a **box** of milk. Then, 1, 2, 3, 4, 5, **six!** BAM!

Oops! Can Max and Ann **fix** this?

Choose the Correct Answer

1. Where are Ann and Max?

   a. at home

   b. in the lab

   c. at camp

2. What happens after Ann adds milk to the pan?

   a. The pan gets hot.

   b. It makes a BAM! noise.

   c. Max goes to the lab.

Word List

Read the words out loud. Then circle the words that end with -*ck* as in **lo<u>ck</u>**.

back	kit	tip	lips	pit	sock
sick	kick	pack	six	sack	box
tick	bad	pick	lock	fix	rock

Word Search

PART A Find and circle the words. The words can be down or across.

box	dock	fox	fix
lock	pack	sack	dim

```
t i c k p a c k
d l o c k f o x
o t o c k d i m
c f i x s a c k
k b o x r o c k
```

Write It

PART B Use the remaining letters to find the answer to the question. Write the answer on the line.

What music do clocks like to play?

Vocabulary Builder

Read each word, its part of speech, and its meaning.

Then write a sentence using the word.

Target Word Read the target words.	Meaning Think about the meanings.	Example Complete each sentence using the target word.
kick (verb)	to strike something or somebody with the foot	I can _____ a football _____ _____ _____
lock (verb)	to fasten something with a key	I would _____ up my _____ _____ _____
pack (verb)	to put objects into a box, case, or bag	In my backpack, I always _____ _____ _____
pick (verb)	to choose something	The next movie I would _____ is _____ _____
sick (adjective)	not feeling well	When I'm _____, I _____ _____ _____

Make Meaning

Tongue Twisters	Word Count: 13

Yackity Yack!

Max **packs** six fat **tack sacks**.

Kids in **socks kick rocks** on **docks**.

Choose the Correct Answer

1. How many sacks does Max pack?

    a. six

    b. three

    c. nine

2. What is in the sacks?

    a. rocks

    b. pots

    c. tacks

Fiction

Word Count: 38

Stinky Socks

Rick sniffs his **socks**. His **socks** stink! In fact, his **socks** make him **sick**! Tim **picks** up Rick's **socks**. Ick! Tim **kicks** Rick's **socks**! Now Rick is not **sick**, and he is not mad at Tim.

"My **socks**!"

Order It

Put the events of the story in the order in which they happen.

1. Number each sentence 1, 2, or 3.

    _____ Tim kicks Rick's socks.

    _____ Rick sniffs his socks.

    _____ Tim picks up Rick's socks.

Choose the Correct Answer

2. Rick is mad at Tim.

    a. true

    b. false

Segment 3

Welcome to Segment 3!

In Segment 3, you'll learn about
s-blends. You'll also study the short
vowels e and u, as well as some
consonants, such as j and w. Finally,
you'll use these skills to read an
inspiring story about a kid who uses
his gardening skills to grow food for
people in need. When you're ready,
just turn the page to get started.

Blends
- s-Blends

Short Vowels
- Short e
- Short u

Consonants
- j, w
- g, y
- v, z, q

In 2016, a California company donated 494,000 pounds of fruits and vegetables to help people in need. That's greater than the weight of two large airplanes!

Word List

Read the words out loud. Then circle the words with **s–blends**.

stick	stack	spot	him	cap	slid
sick	hot	slam	stop	span	sat
spin	sack	sock	tick	slap	slim

> ### REVIEW
> <u>sl</u>im • <u>sp</u>in • <u>st</u>op
>
> Letter **s** often appears with other consonants to form **consonant blends**. The letters in a consonant blend go together, but you can hear the sound each consonant stands for.

Sort It

Read the words in the boxes below. Then write each one under the word that begins with the same consonant blend.

slick	stock	slip	span	stick
slap	stack	slim	spin	slid

1. <u>sl</u>am	2. <u>sp</u>ot	3. <u>st</u>op

Vocabulary Builder

Read each word, its part of speech, and its meaning.

Then write a sentence using the word.

Target Word Read the target words.	Meaning Think about the meanings.	Example Complete each sentence using the target word.
skip (verb)	to leave something out or to pass over	If I had to _____ lunch, I would feel _____ _____
slam (verb)	to close something loudly	I _____ shut _____ _____ _____
snack (noun)	a small, light meal	For a _____ , I eat _____ _____ _____
spot (noun)	a small mark or stain	Something that leaves a _____ on my clothes is _____ _____
stop (verb)	to come to an end	I would like to _____ _____ _____

Fiction

Word Count: 32

Slippery Stan

Stan sits on a **slick** rock. Stan **spots** a fat fish. He licks his lips.

Stan **stands** on the rock and **slips!** He cannot **stop!** Now, Stan is a **slick**, wet cat!

Choose the Correct Answer

1. What happens right *before* Stan licks his lips?

    a. Stan spots a fat fish.

    b. Stan stands up.

    c. Stan slips.

2. How does Stan end up at the end of the story?

    a. with a fat fish

    b. with lots of rocks

    c. as a slick, wet cat

Fiction

Word Count: 33

Colin the Slob

Colin is a **slob**! He **spits** his gum on his desk! He **spills** milk on his **stack** of disks. His socks **stick** on his fan! And Colin's socks **stink**! Colin has to **stop**!

Choose the Correct Answer

1. What makes Colin a slob?

    a. He spits on his dishes.

    b. He spills milk on his stack of disks.

    c. His socks stick to his gum.

2. What sticks on the fan?

    a. socks

    b. pants

    c. gum

Word List

Read the words out loud. Then circle the words with the **short *e* sound** you hear in ***s<u>e</u>t***.

men	pen	man	speck	bed	pet
sled	fad	neck	pat	dim	deck
bat	stem	stop	step	dock	bad

REVIEW

s<u>e</u>t • st<u>e</u>m

These words have the **short *e* vowel sound.** Letter *e* usually stands for the short *e* sound in words with a consonant-vowel-consonant pattern (CVC).

Find It

Read each clue. Then find the word that goes with each clue. Write it on the line. The first one is done for you.

bed	sled	men	stem

step	pet	speck	ten

1. You can slip down a hill with me. _____ sled _____

2. I am 5 + 5. _____

3. I am a cat. _____

4. You can rest on me. _____

5. I am not 1 man, but 2. _____

6. I am a part of a plant. _____

7. I am just a bit. _____

8. I can help you get up to the deck. _____

Vocabulary Builder

Read each word, its part of speech, and its meaning.

Then write a sentence using the word.

Target Word Read the target words.	Meaning Think about the meanings.	Example Complete each sentence using the target word.
bed (noun)	a place where you sleep	I get out of _____ at _____ _____
deck (noun)	the floor of a boat or ship	From the _____ of a ship, I would like to see _____ _____
men (noun)	more than one man	My favorite _____ 's sports team is _____ _____
neck (noun)	the part of your body that joins your head to your shoulders	Around my _____, I can wear _____ _____
ten (adjective)	having the amount of the number 10	Something that is _____ miles away is _____ _____

Fiction

All-U-Can-Fit Tent

Kim packs her **tent** in a **red** backpack. Look at Kim's **tent**! The **tent** is big! Kim can fit a **bed** in the **tent**!

Kim thinks, "It is sad that I cannot fit a **bed** in this **red** backpack."

Choose the Correct Answer

1. Kim packs a tent in the backpack.

    a. true

    b. false

2. Kim's backpack is green.

    a. true

    b. false

Write It

Write a sentence to answer the question.

3. Why doesn't Kim have a bed?

    _____

    _____

Fiction

Word Count: 60

Which Sled Wins?

The **sled** race is on! Six **men** in black tops sit on a black **sled.** The black **sled** is fast.

Ten **men** in **red** tops sit on a **red sled.** The **red sled** is fast. But it is not big. Can the **ten men** fit? Can the **red sled** win? The black **sled** hits a rock! The **red sled** wins!

Choose the Correct Answer

1. Six men ride on the red sled.

    a. true

    b. false

2. Six men sit on the black sled.

    a. true

    b. false

3. The red sled is small.

    a. true

    b. false

4. The red sled is slow.

    a. true

    b. false

Word List

Read the words out loud. Then circle the words with **j** as in **_jet_**.
Underline the words with **w** as in **_win_**.

wick	web	ram	wax	wed	jot
pick	net	jam	sled	tin	win
jet	wet	tax	led	hot	job

Sentence Solver

Use the words in the boxes below to complete each sentence.

jam	jet	wet	jot	win

1. Kim went on a trip in a _____.

2. Sam will _____ the top spot.

3. The cat fell in the tub and is _____.

4. Jim has _____ on a bun for a snack.

5. Get a pen and _____ this on a pad.

Write It

Choose one word from the Sentence Solver activity. Then use it in a sentence.

6. _____

_____

Vocabulary Builder

Read each word, its part of speech, and its meaning.

Then write a sentence using the word.

Target Word Read the target words.	Meaning Think about the meanings.	Example Complete each sentence using the target word.
jam (noun)	a sweet, thick food made from fruit and sugar	My favorite kind of _____ is _____ _____
job (noun)	work that you do to earn money	A _____ I would like to do is _____ _____
web (noun)	a net of sticky, thin threads made by a spider	I've seen a spider _____ in _____ _____
wet (adjective)	covered in liquid	A sport that makes you get_____ _____ is _____ _____
win (verb)	to be the best in a contest or game	I would like to _____ _____ _____

Comic

Word Count: 26

Jen Jets!

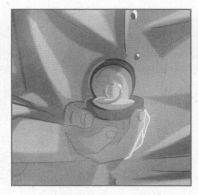

Jen is a **jock**. Jen met
Jin on a run.

Jin asks to wed Jen.

Jen cannot wed yet.
Jen is in a **jam**. Jen **jets!**

Write It

Write a sentence to answer each question.

1. How did Jen meet Jin?

_____

2. Which person is the jock?

_____

3. Why does Jen jet?

_____

Fiction

Word Count: 33

Jed's Jam

Jed is in a cab. Jed's cab is in a bad traffic **jam.** His cab stops. It has no gas left in it. Jed can fix this! Jed can jog to his **job!**

Choose the Correct Answers

1. What are two ways that Jed can travel to work? Choose TWO correct answers.

    a. He can jog.

    b. He can swim.

    c. He can take a cab.

    d. He can fly.

2. What problems does Jed have? Choose TWO correct answers.

    a. His cab is in a traffic jam.

    b. Jed must fix the cab.

    c. Jed must drive the cab.

    d. His cab has no gas left in it.

Nonfiction

Word Count: 52

The Web

The **Web** is not bad! It has a lot of facts. The **Web** has facts on **wax**, jets, pets, and rocks. It can show you jobs, maps, and stocks.

But a lot of **Web** facts can be bad. It is best to stop and check the facts you spot on the **Web**.

Write It

Write a sentence to answer each question.

1. Does the author think the Web is bad?

_____

2. What are two things the Web has facts on?

_____

3. What should you do with facts from the Web?

_____

Fiction

Word Count: 62

Cat in a Well

A sad cat is in a bad jam. It fell in a **well.** The **well** is dim. It is **wet** and slick. The **well** is 24 feet deep. The cat **went** 10 feet in the **well.** Then it slid! The cat cannot hop back to the **well's** rim. The cat is mad! It has sat in the dim **well** for six hours! Help!

Match It

Draw a line from each sentence to its correct answer.

1. At the end of the story, the cat feels _____.

2. The well is _____.

3. The cat has sat in the well for _____.

six hours

wet and slick

mad

Write It

Write a sentence to answer the question.

4. Why is the cat in a bad jam?

_____

Word List

Read the words out loud. Then circle the words with the **short _u_ sound** you hear in **_up_**.

mud	stuck	run	rib	bus	stick
cut	deck	mom	luck	slam	hum
bat	lack	up	ham	rub	duck

Write It

Say the name of each picture. Then write the name of the picture on the line.

1.
_____

4.
_____

7.
_____

2.
_____

5.
_____

8.
_____

3.
_____

6.
_____

9.
_____

Vocabulary Builder

Read each word, its part of speech, and its meaning.

Then write a sentence using the word.

Target Word Read the target words.	Meaning Think about the meanings.	Example Complete each sentence using the target word.
bus (noun)	a large vehicle that people travel on	I've taken a _____ to _____ _____
cut (verb)	to use a knife or scissors to divide something into pieces	Some things that I _____ with scissors are _____. _____
duck (noun)	a bird with webbed feet that swims and feeds in water	A _____ makes a sound like _____ _____
hum (verb)	to sing with your lips closed	I can_____ _____ _____
luck (noun)	something good that happens by chance	I say, "good _____" when _____ _____

Fiction

Word Count: 26

Tuck and the Tub

Brad has Tuck. Tuck is **just** a **pup.**
Tuck **runs** in the **mud.** Yuck! Brad
fills the **tub.** Tuck **jumps** in the **suds.**
"Stop it, Tuck!"

Choose the Correct Answer

1. Which one is the pup?

    a. Tuck

    b. Brad

2. Why does Brad fill the tub?

    a. Tuck runs in the mud.

    b. Tuck jumps in the suds.

Write It

Write a sentence to answer the question.

3. Does Brad seem mad at Tuck? Explain your answer.

Fiction

Word Count: 47

Sunny Side Up

Todd and Wen get **up** at six. Todd wants eggs, ham, and a **cup** of milk. **But** Wen **just** wants a **muffin.**

Todd and Wen hop on a **bus** and head to the **Truck** Stop Inn. They are in **luck!** It has **stuff** that hits the spot!

Choose the Correct Answer

1. Who wants a muffin?

    a. Todd

    b. Wen

2. How do Todd and Wen travel?

    a. They hop on a bus.

    b. They run.

3. Where do Todd and Wen go to eat?

    a. the Truck Stop Inn

    b. a bus stop

Contrasting Short Vowels

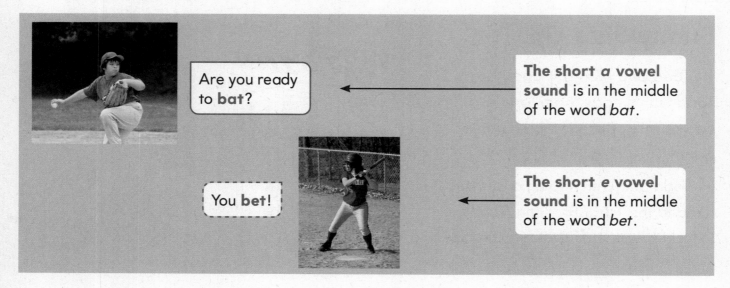

Short Vowel Sounds

Write the letter of the short vowel sound you hear read out loud.

1. n [ ] t
2. n [ ] t
3. m [ ] p
4. m [ ] p

5. b [ ] g
6. b [ ] g
7. f l [ ] p
8. f l [ ] p

9. b [ ] n k
10. b [ ] n k
11. d [ ] s k
12. d [ ] s k

Identify Short Vowels

Read each word. Underline the letter that stands for the vowel sound.

red	rip	dog	fill	truck
cap	bug	map	stop	spin

Sort It

Write each short vowel word in the correct box.

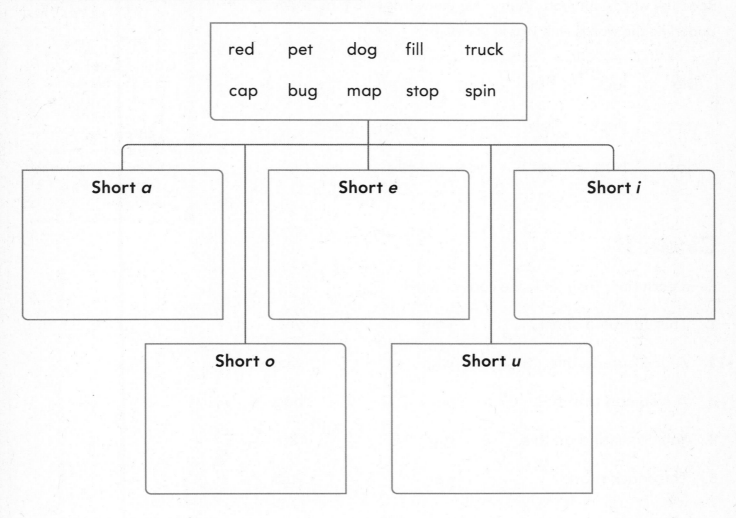

red   pet   dog   fill   truck

cap   bug   map   stop   spin

Short a

Short e

Short i

Short o

Short u

Context Clues

Write the correct word in the blank.

1. Can I _____ your dog? (pet/pot)

2. The kids will _____ in the sand. (dog/dig)

3. Take a ride in the _____ . (truck/track)

4. I drank a _____ of milk. (cup/cap)

5. The dish _____ off the shelf. (fill/fell)

Word List

Read the words out loud. Then circle the words with **g** as in **gas**.
Underline the words with **y** as in **yuck**.

dig	luck	bun	bet	ham	tip
dim	yuck	job	jog	yam	rug
gas	bug	yet	yes	big	run

REVIEW

gas • yuck

- Consonant **g** can stand for the sound you hear at the beginning of the word **gas**.
- Consonant **y** can stand for the sound you hear at the beginning of the word **yuck**.

Circle It

Read each clue. Then circle the correct word.

1. This can be a snack.   yam   yes
2. A dog can do this.   wig   wag
3. A web can trap this.   yet   bug
4. You can stand on this.   rug   dig
5. The snack is bad.   get   yuck

Complete It

Complete each word by filling in the blank with **y** or **g**.
You may use a dictionary for help.

6. di __   9. bi __

7. __ uck   10. __ as

8. __ es

Vocabulary Builder

Read each word, its part of speech, and its meaning.

Then write a sentence using the word.

Target Word Read the target words.	Meaning Think about the meanings.	Example Complete each sentence using the target word.
big (adjective)	large in size	Another animal that is _____ is _____ _____
bug (noun)	a small insect	A _____ that scares me is a _____ _____
rug (noun)	something that covers a floor	The color of a _____ in my house is _____ _____
yes (noun)	a word said to show you agree	I would say, "_____" if someone asked me to _____ _____
yet (adverb)	up until now	A movie I haven't seen _____ is _____ _____

Make Meaning

Got Ya!

Jack and his pals step out to play **tag.**

"Not It!" yells Jack.

"Not It!" yell Lin, Alex, and Jen.

Sol is "It." Sol can run fast. He **tags** Jen. Now Jen is "It." Jen is slick. She is fast. She **tags** Tim. Tim's **legs** are tired. Tim cannot **jog.** Tim has to sit.

"I must quit!" yells Tim.

Choose the Correct Answer

1. Who is "It" first?

    a. Sol

    b. Jen

2. Who is "It" second?

    a. Sol

    b. Jen

Write It

Write a sentence to answer the question.

3. Why does Tim quit?

_____ .

Fiction

Word Count: 47

Peg and the Bug

Gil **jogs** with his **big dog,** Peg. Peg **digs** up **bugs.** Gil yells if Peg brings a **bug** back. Yuck! "Peg, **get** rid of that **bug!**" Gil will not let Peg on his bed. He pushes her off. Peg and the **bug** must nap on the **rug!**

Match It

Write a sentence to answer the question.

1. What does Gil do?   on the rug

2. What does Peg do?   jogs with his dog

3. Where must the bug nap?   digs up bugs

Choose the Correct Answer

4. When does Gil yell?

    a. when Peg naps on the rug

    b. when Peg brings a bug back

Ad

Say Yes!

Yes, you can get the best for less! I sell rock and hip-hop CDs, lots of wigs, cups and mugs, a rare **yak** pendant, a big red and black rug, and more!

Yet, that is not it! I sells **yams**, figs, and plums as well. **Yum!**

2:00 at 5 **Yell** Back Rd.

Match It

Draw a line from each question to its correct answer.

1. What word describes the rug Yasmin is selling?

2. What is one kind of food she sells?

3. What is one kind of music that she sells?

hip-hop

plums

big

Write It

Write a sentence to answer the question.

4. What time is the tag sale?

_____

Advice

Word Count: 41

Yuck!

Dear Kim,

Help! Mom tells me, "Eat **yams**." But yams are **yuck, yuck, yuck!** If I **yell**, "Mom, I hate **yams**," Mom gets mad. **Yet**, if I say, **"Yes!,"** I get sick! Kim, I cannot win! What can I do?

— Yan

Write It

Write a sentence to answer each question.

1. What does Yan think about yams?

    _____

2. What does Mom tell Yan?

    _____

Word List

Read the words out loud. Then circle the words with **q** as in **quiz**. Underline the words with **v** as in **van**. Put a star next to the words that start with **z** as in **zip**.

quit	hip	quack	yet	quiz	jog
van	quick	slam	zap	vat	rap
zip	wick	vet	sock	zag	spin

Sentence Solver

PART A Use the words below to complete each sentence.

mat	van	zip	vet	quiz

1. The cat took a nap on the _____.

2. Did you study for our _____ today?

3. I saw the _____ parked next door.

4. Jon took his dog to the _____.

5. Be sure to _____ up your jacket.

PART B Read each item. Then write your answer on the line.

6. Change just one letter of **quack** to make a new word.

   _____

7. Write a word that rhymes with **zap**.

   _____

Vocabulary Builder

Read each word, its part of speech, and its meaning.

Then write a sentence using the word.

Target Word Read the target words.	Meaning Think about the meanings.	Example Complete each sentence using the target word.
quick (adjective)	fast	A _____ animal is _____ _____ _____
quit (verb)	to stop doing something	Something I have_____ is _____ _____
van (noun)	a small truck shaped like a box	People drive a _____ to ___ _____ _____
vet (noun)	an animal doctor	A _____ can _____ _____ _____
zip (verb)	to move fast	I _____ around town _____ _____ _____

Fiction

Word Count: 50

Quack!

Quinn and I were in my van. Ten ducks sat in the lot. "**Quack, quack, quack!**" went the ducks. The ducks would not **quit.**

"Quinn, I cannot back up!" I said.

Quinn let out a big "**QUACK!**" The ducks ran to the grass. "**Quick**," Quinn said. "You can back up."

Choose the Correct Answer

1. What is the problem in this story?

    a. The van cannot back up.

    b. The ducks ran to the grass.

2. How does Quinn fix the problem?

    a. She quacks.

    b. She backs up the van.

Fiction

Word Count: 53

The Pop Quiz

"There will be a **quick quiz** in class. It is a pop **quiz**," said Miss Ban.

"But you did not tell us about the **quiz!**"

"It is just a **quick quiz** on rocks," she said.

Rocks? Jon is in luck. He has a lot of rocks. Jon got an A on the **quiz!**

Choose the Correct Answer

1. What type of quiz will Miss Ban give the class?

    a. a quiz about ducks

    b. a quiz about rocks

2. Who does well on the quiz?

    a. Miss Ban

    b. Jon

Word Count: 49

Man With a Van

Fast Frank can help you with any job!

- ☑ Need a van?
- ☑ Stuck in the mud?
- ☑ Cannot lift a box?
- ☑ Run out of gas?
- ☑ Bring a cat to the vet?
- ☑ Mend a rip in a vest?

You are in luck! I am the man for the job!

Fast Frank (555) 515-5555

Call Fast Frank, the Man With a Van!
Fast Frank (555) 515–5555

Write It

Write a sentence to answer the question.

1. What are two things Frank can help you with?

_____

_____

_____

_____

Fiction

Word Count: 58

A Trip to the Vet

Val's dog, Socks, is sick. She will not eat. She just naps on a quilt. Val takes Socks in a **van** to **visit** the **vet**. The **vet** gets a pill from his **vest** and hands it to Socks.

The dog pill helps! Socks gets up. She runs to Val and wags. Socks wants a snack! Val is glad!

Choose the Correct Answer

1. What is wrong with Socks?

    a. She has a fever.

    b. She hates the vet.

    c. She will not eat.

2. What does Socks do after she gets the dog pill?

    a. runs to Val

    b. gets sick

    c. visits the vet

Comic

Word Count: 26

Zeb's Gift

Rick naps a lot and has no **zest**. He is sick.

Zeb grabs his pals. They **zip** by Rick's with a gift.

Get well quick, Rick!

Write It

Write a sentence to answer each question.

1. What is wrong with Rick?

_____

2. What do Rick's pals do for him?

_____

Fiction

Zip Up the Bucks!

Scott stuck ten bucks in his backpack. "**Zip** that up, Scott," said Ellen. "I cannot **zip** it. The zipper is stuck."

"Quick, let me help," said Ellen. "OK, it **zips!**"

"Ellen, you are the best!"

Choose the Correct Answer

1. What is the problem in this story?

    a. The zipper is stuck.

    b. Scott can't find his ten bucks.

2. Who fixes the problem?

    a. Scott

    b. Ellen

Contrasting Consonants

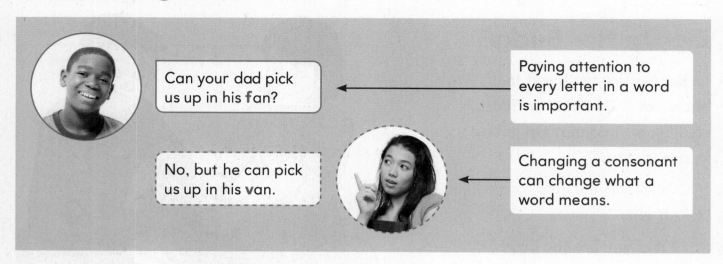

Can your dad pick us up in his **f**an?

Paying attention to every letter in a word is important.

No, but he can pick us up in his **v**an.

Changing a consonant can change what a word means.

Match It

Circle the word you hear read out loud. Listen for the initial consonant sounds.

1. pet   get   3. tin   bin   5. pot   got

2. mat   cat   4. jam   yam   6. nap   tap

Underline It

Underline the word you hear read out loud. Listen for the end consonant sounds.

1. peg   pet   3. hop   hot   5. bib   bid

2. rib   rid   4. ham   hat   6. bag   bad

Sentence Solver

Circle the word that completes the sentence.

1. I drank the hot cocoa from a _____.   pug   mug

2. The player put the basketball through the _____.   net   met

3. My dog likes to _____ a hole for his bones.   big   dig

4. There was a very _____ storm last night.   bad   dad

5. The big _____ crawled across the wall.   bud   bug

6. My uncle is the pilot of a _____.   yet   jet

7. The team rode to the game in a _____.   van   ran

8. Do you want a dog or a cat for a _____?   get   pet

Word Hunt

Use the words from the box to complete the sentences. You will not use every word.

rat	bib	lip	bid	ran	dog
peg	pen	lap	pot	jog	hot

1. The baby wore a _____

2. I write with a _____

3. The sun was very _____

4. To get exercise, I went for a _____

5. I held my new kitten in my _____

6. I hung my backpack on the _____

Segment 4

Welcome to Segment 4!

By now, you've mastered single consonants and short vowels. In Segment 4, you'll move on to double consonants and final blends. You'll also read an incredible story about dogs—and how they use their powerful sense of smell to help humans. Ready? Let's get started!

Consonants •————————

- Double Consonants (*ff*, *ll*, *ss*)

Blends •————————

- Final Blends

Dogs have an incredible sense of smell. One reason for this super power? Snot! The mucus in a dog's nose helps the animal smell by capturing scent particles in the air.

Word List

Read the words out loud. Then circle the words that end with two of the same consonants.

stuff	quick	spin	men	skit	snack
stock	kiss	sniff	sell	skill	sick
spell	skull	cuff	kid	mess	spill

REVIEW

sn**iff** • sku**ll** • me**ss**

When two of the same consonants appear together, they usually stand for one sound.

Replace It

Replace the underlined letter or letters with **ff**, **ll**, or **ss** to make a new word. The first one is done for you.

ff	ll	ss

1. wi<u>ck</u> _____will_____

2. pa<u>n</u> _____

3. se<u>ts</u> _____

4. le<u>t</u> _____

5. stu<u>b</u> _____

6. spe<u>ck</u> _____

7. spi<u>n</u> _____

8. ski<u>m</u> _____

9. me<u>t</u> _____

10. sni<u>p</u> _____

Vocabulary Builder

Read each word, its part of speech, and its meaning.

Then write a sentence using the word.

Target Word Read the target words.	Meaning Think about the meanings.	Example Complete each sentence using the target word.
cuff (noun)	the end part of a sleeve	I would roll up my _____ when I _____ _____
fuss (noun)	more talk or activity than is necessary	I make a _____ when _____ _____
kiss (noun)	a touch with the lips, as in a greeting	Someone who might greet me with a _____ is _____ _____
less (adverb)	not so much	I want to spend _____ time _____ _____
mess (noun)	things that are not neat	When I see a _____, I _____ _____

Fiction

Word Count: 36

Bill's Boss

Bill does not like his job. His **boss**, Ann, gets mad a lot. Ann **yells** at the **staff**.

Bill quits his job. At his next job, Bill is the **boss**. Will he **yell?** Time will **tell!**

Write It

Write a sentence to answer each question.

1. Why doesn't Bill like his job?

   _____

   _____

2. Who is the boss at Bill's next job?

   _____

   _____

Science Nonfiction

Word Count: 68

Shake, Rattle, and Buzz

A snake **will** bask in the sun on hot rocks and **cliffs**. It **will** sit on the sand and in **grass** as **well**. It **will** make a **fuss** to **tell** you to back **off**. As a **bluff**, it can **hiss** and **puff** up.

A rattlesnake has a tail that **will buzz** and rattle. If you hear a **buzz**, do not panic and **yell**. Just get past it fast!

Match It

Draw a line from each question to its correct answer.

1. Where does a snake bask?

2. How does a snake tell you to back off?

3. What can its tail do?

buzz and rattle

hiss and puff up

hot rocks and cliffs

Choose the Correct Answer

4. What should you do if you hear a snake rattle?

    a. panic and yell

    b. get past it fast

Word List

Read the words out loud. Then circle the words that end with any of the following **final blends**: *sk*, *st*, *ft*, *lp*, *ct*.

lips	rest	fact	beds	ask	quick
desk	gift	snug	risk	deck	mask
list	spill	help	step	test	mats

Word Search

Find the words in the puzzle. Then circle them. The words can be down or across.

risk	**help**	**act**	**west**
mask	**nest**	**fast**	**gift**

```
f  u  b  r  z  d  y  g  q  c  k
a  l  q  w  j  r  q  i  z  j  e
s  j  h  e  l  p  m  f  b  y  b
t  m  a  s  k  w  z  t  p  q  p
j  z  o  t  q  n  b  z  y  a  i
q  a  r  d  w  e  n  l  k  s  q
z  c  j  r  i  s  k  m  n  l  c
u  t  q  w  c  t  h  z  w  m  y
```

Vocabulary Builder

Read each word, its part of speech, and its meaning.

Then write a sentence using the word.

Target Word Read the target words.	Meaning Think about the meanings.	Example Complete each sentence using the target word.
act (verb)	to perform in a play or movie	I would like to _____ the part of _____ _____
best (adjective)	better than everything else	The _____ film I've seen this year is _____ _____
fast (adverb)	moving in a quick way	An animal that runs _____ is _____ _____
mask (noun)	a covering worn to hide or protect the face	I would wear a _____ if _____ _____
stamp (noun)	something you stick on a letter to pay for postage	One picture on a _____ is _____ _____

Fiction

Word Count: 57

Stan's Quest

Stan went to get a pen in his **desk.** He found a big black and red bug in his **desk** instead. That bug had lots of legs!

Stan is now on a **quest.** His **task** is to get rid of the **pests** in his house. Stan will not **rest** a bit until he zaps every **last** bug!

Order the Events

Put the events of the story in the order in which they happen.

1. Number each sentence 1, 2, or 3.

    _____ Stan found a bug in his desk.

    _____ Stan is now on a quest.

    _____ Stan went to get a pen in his desk.

Write It

Write a sentence to answer the question.

2. When will Stan rest?

    _____

    _____

Comic

Word Count: 26

A Strong Wind

Choose the Correct Answer

1. What is too brisk?

    a. the mess

    b. the gust of wind

2. What will they use to pick up the mess?

    a. plastic bags

    b. a backpack

Recognizing & Using Contractions

Do not bother *John's* dog. **It is** asleep.

Don't bother *Lisa's* cat. **It's** asleep, too.

A **contraction** is formed by combining two words, with some letters left out. An apostrophe takes the place of the missing letters.

An apostrophe can also show possession. Do not confuse *possessives* with contractions.

Write It

Write each contraction next to its correct word pair.

| won't | didn't | he's | they'll | wasn't |

1. he is _____

2. they will _____

3. was not _____

4. did not _____

5. will not _____

Write It

Read each contraction. Write the words that form the contraction.

1. hadn't _____

2. it's _____

3. doesn't _____

4. she's _____

5. they've _____

6. aren't _____

7. we'll _____

8. don't _____

9. they're _____

10. we're _____

Analyze Words

Circle each word with an apostrophe. Write *P* if it is a possessive and *C* if it is a contraction.

1. We haven't eaten dinner yet. _____

2. I lost my friend's computer. _____

3. You can't swim during a storm. _____

4. She's home sick today. _____

5. Our school's band won the contest. _____

6. I don't want to see that movie. _____

Use Contractions

Write a contraction in the blank to complete each sentence.

1. I _____ spread rumors. (will not)

2. _____ be here soon. (She will)

3. _____ go to the park. (Let us)

4. I think _____ going on a trip. (he is)

5. I _____ know the answer. (do not)

6. _____ your brother? (Where is)

Understanding Syllables

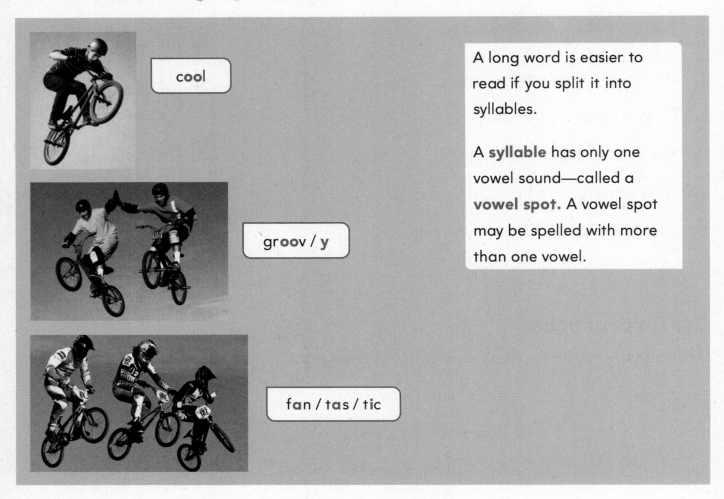

cool

groov / y

fan / tas / tic

A long word is easier to read if you split it into syllables.

A **syllable** has only one vowel sound—called a **vowel spot.** A vowel spot may be spelled with more than one vowel.

Identify Vowel Spots

Read each word. Underline each vowel spot in the word.

1. truck

2. limitless

3. robin

4. happen

5. plastic

6. habit

7. handful

8. cabinet

9. mess

10. dust

11. talentless

12. bonds

Sort Words

Write each word from the left page in the correct box.

One Syllable	Two Syllables	Three Syllables

Split It

Draw a line to divide each word into syllables. Then write the syllables.
The first one is done for you.

1. pan|ic
          pan   ic

2. traffic
   _____   _____

3. upset
   _____   _____

4. helpful
   _____   _____

5. endless
   _____   _____

6. napkin
   _____   _____

7. sandwich
   _____   _____

8. timid
   _____   _____

Segments 5–6

Welcome to Segments 5–6!

Congratulations—you've made it to Segments 5–6! Here you'll focus on blends. This includes *l*-blends, *r*-blends, and two- and three-letter blends. You'll also study closed syllables. Finally, you'll use these skills to read two inspiring stories about people who are helping to protect bees and other creatures. Now, turn the page to get started!

Blends

- *l*-Blends
- *r*-Blends
- Two- and Three-Letter Blends

Syllables

- Closed Syllables

As bees fly, they beat their wings about 13,000 times per minute. The movement is so fast that it causes a buzzing sound. Buzz!

Word List

Read the words out loud. Then circle the words with *l-blends*.

cliff	clap	glad	snap	block
sniff	pack	kick	blog	glass
clock	laptop	stock	magnet	stack
click	black	club	insist	pick

REVIEW

<u>b</u>lack • <u>c</u>lub • <u>g</u>lad

Letter *l* often appears with other consonants to form **consonant blends.** The letters in a consonant blend go together, but you can hear the sound each consonant stands for.

Sort It

Read the words below. Then write each one under the word that begins with the same consonant blend.

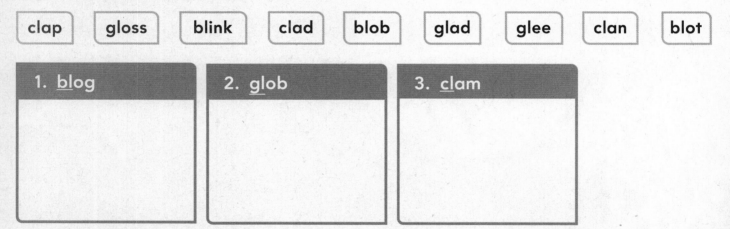

| clap | gloss | blink | clad | blob | glad | glee | clan | blot |

1. <u>bl</u>og	2. <u>gl</u>ob	3. <u>cl</u>am

Write It

Read each item. Write your answer on the blank.

4. Add one letter to the beginning of **lip** to make a new word.

_____

5. Add one letter to the beginning of **lad** to make a new word.

_____

Vocabulary Builder

Read each word, its part of speech, and its meaning.

Then write a sentence using the word.

Target Word Read the target words.	Meaning Think about the meanings.	Example Complete each sentence using the target word.
block (noun)	a piece of something hard	A child can use a _____ to build _____ _____
cliff (noun)	a high, steep rock face	From the top of a _____, you might see _____ _____
club (noun)	a group of people who meet to share an interest	I would like to join a _____ that _____ _____
flag (noun)	a cloth with a pattern that stands for a country	I've seen a _____ on a pole at _____ _____
glad (adjective)	pleased or happy	Someone who makes me feel ____ _____ is _____ _____

Word Count: 75

Blog Tips

What is a **blog?** You can **click** to get to a **blog** on the Web. In fact, **"blog"** stands for "Web log." A **blog** is a log kept on the Web. A **blog** can be on lots of fun topics. You can **blab** on a band, a **class**, a pet—whatever!

If you get a **blog,** just tell stuff you would be **glad** to tell Mom and Dad. Anyone on the Web can read it!

Write It

Write a sentence to answer each question.

1. What does "blog" stand for?

   _____

2. Who can read a blog?

   _____

Blog

Our Camp Blog

◀ ▶ C

| Home | | Stories | | Sports | | Music |

Cliff and Trent's Camp Blog

Fun stuff we did at Camp Black.

1. Went on a bus trip.
2. Found **plums** and figs.
3. Dug for **clams** in Sunset Bay.
4. Had a picnic at Red Fox **Bluff**.
5. Had a quick swim **class**.

Write It

Write a sentence to answer each question.

1. What is the name of the camp?

    _____

2. What did Cliff and Trent find?

    _____

3. Where did Cliff and Trent have a picnic?

    _____

Word List

Read the words out loud. Then circle the words with **r-blends**.

crust	frost	frog	crab	rust	brick
crop	class	brim	cross	skill	scab
fast	blog	skim	brag	blast	brass

REVIEW

brim • crab • frost

Letter **r** often appears with other consonants to form **consonant blends**. The letters in a consonant blend go together, but you can hear the sound each consonant stands for.

All Mixed Up

Unscramble the words to complete each sentence.

fret	brim	crop	frog	brag
crib	bricks	frost	brass	crab

1. The trumpet is _____ . **sabrs**

2. A _____ has legs and a shell. **abcr**

3. A _____ hops and likes to get wet. **rfgo**

4. Fill the milk to the _____ of the glass. **mbir**

5. They will _____ if they do well on the test. **grba**

6. Do not _____ ! It will be OK! **erft**

7. He will plant the _____ . **proc**

8. There is _____ on the grass. **rfsto**

9. The cabin is made of logs, not _____ . **kcrisb**

10. My sis is in her _____ . **ricb**

Vocabulary Builder

Read each word, its part of speech, and its meaning.
Then write a sentence using the word.

Target Word Read the target words.	Meaning Think about the meanings.	Example Complete each sentence using the target word.
brag (verb)	to talk about yourself in a way that is too proud	Something I could _____ about is _____ _____
brim (noun)	the wider part that sticks out of a hat	People wear hats with a _____ to _____ _____
crop (noun)	a plant such as corn or wheat that farmers grow and sell	Farmers grow a _____ like _____ _____
cross (verb)	to go from one side of a place to the other	On the way to school, I _____ _____ _____
frog (noun)	a small animal with smooth skin that lives in or near water	The _____ uses its strong back legs _____ _____

Fiction

Word Count: 54

The Frilly Hat

Granddad picks up a lot of odd stuff in junk shops. And then he sends it to me! I just got a hat as a gift. The hat is tan. It has a big **brim** with red velvet pompoms stuck on it. And the **brim** has **frills** as well. Yuck! What was Granddad thinking?!

Choose the Correct Answer

1. Who picks up stuff in junk shops?

    a. the girl in the purple vest

    b. Granddad

Write It

Write a sentence to answer the question.

2. What does the hat look like? List three details.

_____

_____

Comic

Word Count: 51

Crazy Cuts

CAM: I must get my hair cut. It's puffy on top and has lots of **frizz**. I cannot fix it. I am sick of it. Should I get a buzz cut and **crop** it all off? Can you help me pick a cut?

CASS: Not a problem. Let me at it!

Write It

Write a sentence to answer each question.

1. Why does Cam get her hair cut?

_____

2. Look at the second picture. How does Cam's hair look after it is cut?

_____

Word List

Read the words out loud. Then circle the words that begin with **two-letter blends.** Underline the words that begin with **three-letter blends.**

luck	split	sprint	strip	list	less
laptop	struck	scrap	strap	swim	stress
lips	laps	insist	twist	denim	strum

Sentence Solver

Use the words below to complete each sentence.

twin	strap	swim	sprint	split	scrub

1. A _____ is a quick run.

2. Brock will _____ the snack with me. I will have a bit, and he will have a bit!

3. I will have to _____ my pants to get the mud out.

4. I have a _____. He is just like me!

5. Quin has a _____ on his bag.

6. If it is hot out, we can _____.

Vocabulary Builder

Read each word, its part of speech, and its meaning.

Then write a sentence using the word.

Target Word Read the target words.	Meaning Think about the meanings.	Example Complete each sentence using the target word.
scrub (verb)	to clean something by rubbing it	In the kitchen, I might _____ _____ _____
split (verb)	divide into two or more groups	One thing I _____ with a friend is _____ _____
strap (noun)	a strong band that is attached to a bag or shoe	One kind of clothing that has a _____ is _____ _____
swim (verb)	to move in water with your arms and legs	I can _____ at _____ _____ _____
twist (verb)	to turn, wind, or bend	I can _____ _____ _____

Fiction

Word Count: 48

The Grill Is Hot!

I **grab** a rib from the **grill.** It is still hot. It is too hot! I let it **drop. Splat!**

I better **scrub** it up before Mom gets back! This is **grim.** Mom will get upset if she sees that big **black** and red spot on her rug.

Choose the Correct Answer

1. Why does the girl drop the rib?

   a. It is hot.

   b. Mom is not back.

2. How will Mom feel when she sees the spot on her rug?

   a. happy

   b. upset

Fiction

Word Count: 66

Drums Rock!

Granddad got Greg a **drum** set as a gift. But Greg's dad is **strict.** He will not let Greg keep it. Greg's dad cannot stand the racket. But Greg's mom has a **plan.**

"Greg, you can get an air guitar instead," she says with a **grin.**

Mom **strums** a bit. Greg just gets mad at his mom's bad plan. Greg **grabs** his **drumsticks** and stomps out!

Choose the Correct Answer

1. What does Granddad give Greg?

    a. a racket

    b. a drum set

2. What does Greg think of Mom's plan?

    a. It is a bad plan.

    b. It makes him happy.

Apply the Strategy

Word List

Read the words out loud. Then circle the words with two syllables.

plastic	jacket	traffic	king	facts
blink	stack	planet	plans	limit
fantastic	draft	stung	fans	stick
hundred	pocket	drastic	habit	acts

REVIEW

- Finding the syllables in a word can help you figure out how to read it. A **closed syllable** ends in a consonant. It usually has a short vowel sound.
- When there are two consonants in the middle of a word, you usually split the word between them. Example: *blan|ket*.
- When there is just one consonant in the middle of a word, try splitting after it. Example: *hab|it*.

Split It

PART A Circle the vowel spots in each word. Then draw a line to split the words into syllables. Write the syllables on the lines. The first one is done for you.

1. pic|nic ___pic___ ___nic___
2. traf|fic _____ _____
3. rap|id _____ _____
4. jack|et _____ _____
5. tick|et _____ _____
6. dras|tic _____ _____
7. plas|tic _____ _____
8. fan|tas|tic _____ _____ _____
9. hun|dred _____ _____
10. lim|it _____ _____

PART B Choose two words from the activity above and write a sentence using each one.

11. _____
12. _____

Vocabulary Builder

Read each word, its part of speech, and its meaning.
Then write a sentence using the word.

Target Word Read the target words.	Meaning Think about the meanings.	Example Complete each sentence using the target word.
blanket (noun)	a thick covering for a bed	I use a _____ when _____ _____
contest (noun)	a competition	The last _____ I entered was _____ _____
dentist (noun)	someone whose job is to treat people's teeth	People see a _____ to _____ _____
hundred (adjective)	having the amount of the number 100	Something I can do a _____ times is _____ _____
insist (verb)	to demand something firmly	I _____ that _____ _____ _____

Fiction

Word Count: 82

Drastic Measures

It is 7:00, and Jeff has a basketball **ticket** in his **pocket**. His **ticket** is for a **fantastic** spot in the front row. It cost Jeff a **hundred** bucks!

Jeff has to get there fast! He gets in a cab, but his cab gets stuck in **traffic**! Jeff has his cab stop and he gets out. "This is **drastic**," Jeff says. He runs **seven** blocks. But Jeff is in luck! He gets there just in time to see a **fantastic** three-point **basket**!

Write It

Write a sentence to answer each question.

1. Where is Jeff going?

   _____

2. Why does Jeff think he is going to be late?

   _____

3. What does Jeff see when he arrives?

   _____

Word Count: 52

Fantastic Deals

Get **tickets** at
555-6780
(Tickets subject to tax)

HOT DEALS on **Fantastic** Trips!

Jump on a tram and **visit** San Francisco's best spots!

- Step back in time and **visit** the Mission **District**
- Stop off at the **public** markets
- Have a **picnic** in the **Sunset District**
- **Visit** the inns in Nob Hill

Choose the Correct Answer

1. What does the ad give **the most** information about?

    a. public markets

    b. picnics

    c. the best spots in San Francisco

2. How can you get tickets?

    a. call 555–6780

    b. go to a public market

    c. just visit San Francisco

Write It

Write a sentence to answer the question.

3. What is one reason to visit San Francisco?

_____

Read 180 Resources

Additional Fluency Practice and Support

Goals and Achievements

Dictation

Write the sounds, words, or sentences you hear.

Sounds

1. _____   3. _____   5. _____

2. _____   4. _____   6. _____

Words

1. _____   4. _____   7. _____

2. _____   5. _____   8. _____

3. _____   6. _____   9. _____

Sentences

1. _____

_____

2. _____

_____

3. _____

_____

4. _____

_____

5. _____

_____

Dictation

Write the sounds, words, or sentences you hear.

Sounds

1. _____ 3. _____ 5. _____

2. _____ 4. _____ 6. _____

Words

1. _____ 4. _____ 7. _____

2. _____ 5. _____ 8. _____

3. _____ 6. _____ 9. _____

Sentences

1. _____

_____

2. _____

_____

3. _____

_____

4. _____

_____

5. _____

_____

Glossary

act (verb) to perform in a play or movie
My friend will act in the lead role of the school play.

am (verb) the form of the verb to be that is used with I
I am happy when I am in nature.

at (preposition) in a particular place
The kids at the park played basketball.

bad (adjective) not good or not nice
After a bad day, I listen to soothing music.

ban (verb) to forbid something
My parents ban video games on weeknights.

bat (noun) a long piece of wood used for hitting a baseball
The player hit the ball into the stands with her bat.

bats (noun) small, furry animals that fly mostly at night
Bats can sleep upside down.

bed (noun) a place where you sleep
I go to bed early every night.

best (adjective) better than everything else
The best way to travel overseas is by plane.

big (adjective) large in size
The big tent can fit many people.

bit (verb) past tense of bite; to have cut something with your teeth
Yesterday, the dog bit the shoe.

blanket (noun) a thick covering for a bed
You can add an extra blanket to the bed if you are cold.

block (noun) a piece of something hard
The young boy added a wooden block to his toy fort.

box (noun) a container with four flat sides
She stores her baseball cards in a box.

brag (verb) to talk about yourself in a way that is too proud
He likes to brag about all the trophies he has won.

brim (noun) the wider part that sticks out of a hat
The brim helps shade her face from the sun.

bug (noun) a small insect
The bug crawls from the grass to the flower.

bus (noun) a large vehicle that people pay to travel on
We take the bus to travel across town.

cabs (noun) cars that take people places for a fee
They rode in cabs to get from one place to another.

can (verb) to be able to do something
I can speak two languages.

cap (noun) a soft hat with a peak at the front
She wears a cap when she hikes.

caps (noun) small hats
The baseball players wear blue caps.

cat (noun) a small animal with fur and claws, often kept as a pet
The cat plays with yarn.

cliff (noun) a high, steep rock face
The rock climbers reached the top of the cliff.

club (noun) a group of people who meet to share an interest
The school has a club for students who enjoy robotics.

contest (noun) a competition
The winner of the contest will get a medal.

crop (noun) a plant such as corn or wheat that farmers grow and sell
The farm had a new crop of potatoes this year.

cross (verb) to go from one side of a place to the other
She will cross the street to get to the store.

cuff (noun) the end part of a sleeve
He folded his cuff when he washed his hands so it wouldn't get wet.

cut (verb) to use a knife or scissors to divide something into pieces
She will cut paper in many colors for an art project.

deck (noun) the floor of a boat or ship
The passengers on the deck waved to the people on land.

dentist (noun) someone whose job is to treat people's teeth
I went to the dentist because I had a toothache.

dim (adjective) not very bright
He lit candles to brighten the dim room.

duck (noun) a bird with webbed feet that swims and feeds in water
A duck can both swim and fly.

fan (noun) an object for moving air around to cool you
You can turn the fan on to cool down the room.

fast (adverb) moving in a quick way
He moved as fast as he could through the obstacle course.

fit (verb) to be the right size or shape
The shoes are too small, so they do not fit.

flag (noun) a cloth with a pattern that stands for a country
The child waves a flag during the parade.

frog (noun) a small animal with smooth skin that lives in or near water
The frog often visits the pond in the backyard.

fuss (noun) more talk or activity than is necessary
My aunt likes to make a fuss when I visit by cooking a big dinner.

glad (adjective) pleased or happy
I am glad that you can go to the movie theater with me.

had (verb) past tense of have: to possess something
I had a key to the house, but I lost it.

hat (noun) an item of clothing worn on the head
She wears a hat to keep her head warm.

hid (verb) past tense of hide: to keep something from sight
The dog hid under the bed when it thundered last night.

hit (verb) to strike something with your hand or with a tool
He can hit the ball with the tennis racket.

hop (verb) to move with short jumps or leaps
The kangaroo will hop to move forward.

hot (adjective) having a high temperature
The cup became hot when I poured the tea into it.

hum (verb) to sing with your lips closed
You can hum to the song even if you don't know the words.

hundred (adjective) having the amount of the number 100
One hundred people showed up to the outdoor concert.

insist (verb) to demand something firmly
My grandmother will insist that we stay for lunch.

jam (noun) a sweet, thick food made from fruit and sugar
He often eats jam on toast for breakfast.

job (noun) work that you do to earn money
Her mom has a job as a doctor.

kick (verb) to strike something or somebody with the foot
The player will try to kick the ball into the goal.

kiss (verb) to touch with the lips, as in a greeting
I always kiss my dog before we leave the apartment.

kit (noun) a set of tools or things used for a certain purpose
The first-aid kit includes bandages.

less (adverb) not so much
The apple costs less than a bag of oranges.

lid (noun) a cover for a pot or a box
When you remove the lid, you can smell the sauce.

lit (verb) past tense of light: to start something burning
My mom lit a fire when it snowed last month.

lock (verb) to fasten something with a key
He uses the key to lock the door.

luck (noun) something good that happens by chance
With luck, I will get the lead role in the play.

mad (adjective) very angry
I get mad when my sister takes things without asking.

man (noun) an adult male person
The man wore a green tie.

map (noun) a drawing of an area
You can use a map to find the closest road.

mask (noun) a covering worn to hide or protect the face
The costume includes a superhero mask and cape.

mat (noun) a piece of thick material that covers part of a floor
Wipe your shoes on the mat before entering the home.

men (noun) adult males
The men in my family are tall.

mess (noun) things that are not neat
She made a mess when she spilled the paint on the floor.

met (verb) came face to face with someone
Last week, I met my friend at the mall.

mix (verb) to put different things together
When making a cake, I mix the ingredients together in a bowl.

mom (noun) informal; a word that means mother
The boy's mom takes him to school every morning.

naps (noun) short periods of sleep
The dog takes naps every afternoon.

neck (noun) the part of your body that joins your head to your shoulders
I often wear a scarf around my neck when it's cold.

nose (noun) the part of your face you use to smell
Sometimes, a dog's nose can smell things that are over ten miles away.

not (adverb) at no time or in no way
I do not like to get soaked in the rain.

pack (verb) to put objects into a box, case, or bag
I will pack a blanket for the picnic.

pan (noun) a round metal pot used for cooking
He will cook the eggs in a pan.

pet (noun) a tame animal
They have a bird as a pet.

pick (verb) to choose something
I always pick chocolate ice cream over the other flavors.

pin (noun) a short, thin piece of metal with a sharp point
You can use a pin to hang the poster.

pit (noun) a hole in the ground made by digging
They had to dig a pit before building the house.

quick (adjective) fast
I took a quick shower because I did not have much time.

quit (verb) to stop doing something
He will quit the swim team because he hurt his shoulder.

ram (noun) a male sheep
A ram has curved horns.

ran (verb) past tense of run; moved very quickly, using the legs
Yesterday, I ran around the track five times.

rap (noun) a kind of music with words that are spoken in time with the music
My sister likes to dance to rap.

rib (noun) one of the 12 pairs of curved bones in the chest
He hurt his rib when he fell off his bike.

rug (noun) something that covers a floor
There is a rug under the sofa.

sad (adjective) unhappy
The kid felt sad when he moved away from his friends.

scrub (verb) to clean something by rubbing it
You must scrub the dish to remove the food that is stuck on it.

sick (adjective) not feeling well
I usually eat soup when I am sick.

six (adjective) having the amount of the number 6
I started playing the flute six months ago.

skip (verb) to leave something out or to pass over
He may skip practice if he has a test the next day.

slam (verb) to close something loudly
If you slam the door, the baby will wake up.

snack (noun) a small, light meal
Eating a light snack before studying helps me focus.

split (verb) divide into two or more groups
I split the apple in half to share it with my friend.

spot (noun) a small mark or stain
There is a dark spot on her backpack where her pen leaked.

stamp (noun) something you stick on a letter to pay for postage
You must put a stamp on the envelope before you can mail it.

stop (verb) to come to an end
We will stop practicing when we get the song right.

strap (noun) a strong band that is attached to a bag or shoe
When I tried to lift the heavy bag, its strap broke.

sun (noun) the star that gives us light and warmth
The sun is shining brightly today.

swim (verb) to move in water with your arms and legs
We swim in the community pool when the weather is warm.

tan (adjective) a light, yellow-brown color
The leather bag is tan.

ten (adjective) having the amount of the number 10
There are ten eggs left in the carton because I ate two for breakfast.

tiger (noun) a big, striped, wild cat found in Asia
A tiger has black stripes.

tip (noun) the end of something
She sharpens the tip of her pencil before sketching.

top (noun) the highest point or part
They climb to the top of the hill every day.

twist (verb) to turn, wind, or bend
He might twist his ankle if he runs up the rocky path.

van (noun) a small truck shaped like a box
My parents' van can fit six of my teammates.

vet (noun) an animal doctor
We took our bird to the vet when it hurt its wing.

web (noun) a net of sticky, thin threads made by a spider
The spider's web can catch flies.

wet (adjective) covered in liquid
They got wet in the rain after forgetting their umbrellas.

win (verb) to be the best in a contest or game
The team will win if they practice a lot before the big game.

yes (adverb) a word said to show you agree
Yes, I can help you with the assignment.

yet (adverb) up until now
A baby has not yet learned to walk.

zip (verb) to move fast
The train will zip by in five minutes, so we must hurry.

Word Count: 118

Can You Nap?

PART 1

Zzz. Nap time! How do you nap? Can you stand and nap? A horse can. Can you nap at noon? A man can.

Can you nap on a mat? This tan cat can. He can nap on a tan mat.

PART 2

Can you nap and nap all day? A bat and a rat can.

Can you nap upside down? A bat can! Can a rat nap like this tan bat? No. But a rat can nap upright like a cat.

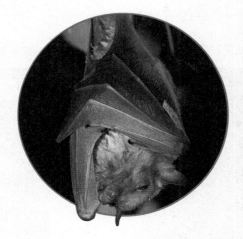

PART 3

Can you nap on land? Horses, cats, bats, and rats can.

Can you nap at sea? An otter can. Can you nap and fly? Surprisingly, this bird can!

An animal can nap on a cap. Can you?

Comic | # Look! Nat Can Do That!

PART 1

PART 2

PART 3

Word Count: 217

Word Count: 178

This Kid Did It!

PART 1

This kid is Ian. He sees a spot with rocks. Can the spot be a garden? It can! But Ian must fix it.

Ian works step by step. First, he gets rid of the rocks. He stacks them in bins.

Then he digs ten pits. He slips seeds in the pits.

Can they grow? They can!

PART 2

Ian heard of some kids. They go to bed hungry. It made him sad.

"I can help," he said. "I can grow food. I can pick it. I can pack it up in bins. They can take the supplies they need. This plan will win!"

He set to it. It was a big job. But he did not stop.

PART 3

Ian had lots of food to dig. He had to get help.

He met some kids. "Can you help with my goal?" he said.

"Yes," they said. "It can be fun!" The kids packed bins. The bins had yams and kale.

Ian and his pals did not quit. They did it! They fed others. It was a big hit.

Fiction

Word Count: 121

Lin and Rex

PART 1

Lin is at a hip-hop show. She is a big fan of Lil Mac.

Lin rubs her dog, Rex.

"Good pup!" she tells him.

Rex smells Lin. Sniff! Sniff! Rex responds and barks.

Something is very wrong!

"I need some help!" yells Lin.

PART 2

Lin rests.

"Can I call for help?" a man asks.

"Yes," Lin tells him. "My brain can get stuck. I can have a seizure. If I lose control, I can slip. But my dog Rex helps me."

PART 3

Soon, Lin gets help.

"Rex has the best nose," insists Lin. "He can sense if I will slip. He barks to tell me."

"So, how are you?" a man asks. It is Lil Mac!

"Much better!" admits Lin.

Word Count: 187

A Big Yes to Less Plastic

PART 1

Plastic trash is bad for the environment. People drop it in the water. They drop plastic cups and lids, too. Animals live in the water. They get stuck in globs of plastic. Frogs and crabs can snack on it. Plastic can kill them.

Can this be stopped? Yes, it can!

PART 2

Nzambi Matee lives in Kenya. She looks at the water. She sees plastic. A lot of it! It snags fish. It snags crabs. They get stuck. Yuck! Matee got mad. What can fix it?

She had an idea. She started a company. It makes bricks. It transforms trash. Her staff picks up trash. They cut it up. They mix it with sand. They put it in the sun. The staff is fast. They make lots of bricks.

PART 3

Matee is not alone. Ocean Sole has big plans. Staff scan the sea. They pick up flip-flops. They pack them in big bags. Staff cut them up. They dab them with glue. They press them. They cut the big slabs. It creates big art. See that big cat there? It is made of flip-flops!

Nonfiction **Just Call Moz**

PART 1

PART 2

PART 3

Word Count: 198

from

Friends: True Stories of Extraordinary Animal Friendships

by Catherine Thimmesh

When the old orangutan at Zoo World in Florida lost her mate, she was listless and would barely eat. Workers worried that she might very well lose her will to live. So they brought a new companion—a stray tabby cat—to her enclosure; first just outside the fence, then in. The two became instant and inseparable friends. For nearly four years, Tonda the orangutan and TK the cat lived side by side—eating, playing, sleeping—until Tonda died of old age. But for four years, both were comforted and content.

orangutan   a large ape with long, red-brown fur and long arms

listless   tired and not interested

enclosure   an area closed in by a fence or wall

inseparable   not wanting to be apart

Summarize

When you **summarize** a text, you use your own words to tell the most important ideas of the text.

Complete the sentences in the boxes below to write a summary for this text. One is done for you. Then combine all the important ideas to write a summary of the text.

First Important Idea:

After an orangutan at Zoo World lost her mate, _____

Second Important Idea:

Workers helped the orangutan by _____

Third Important Idea:

The orangutan and cat _____

Fourth Important Idea:

For four years, the animals comforted each other. _____

SUMMARY

_____

_____

_____

_____

_____

Nonfiction

from

Making a Change:
Tips From an Underage Overachiever
by Bilaal Rajan

I want kids to find their passion, take action, and know that they can do amazing things and make a difference in the lives of others. It's not difficult. If you believe in your cause, and you know that what you are doing is right, you will be able to raise funds, and you should do it. Never lose confidence. Everyone has to find their passion. It may be fund-raising to help kids on the other side of the world; it may be helping animals, helping the elderly in nursing homes, helping the

physically challenged—there are hundreds of worthy causes. I have concentrated on helping kids. I feel kids need to help other kids. Children are the creators and leaders of our future. I believe that there should be equality and fairness for all children.

passion	a very strong feeling
cause	an aim or principle for which people fight, raise money, and draw attention to
worthy	having value or merit

Identify Main Idea and Details

The **main idea** is the most important idea in an article. It is what the text is mostly about. **Details** support the main idea by telling more about it.

Read the main idea of "Making a Change: Tips From an Underage Overachiever" below. Then answer the questions about details.

Main Idea	Details
According to Bilaal Rajan, it's not difficult to make a difference in people's lives.	1. What does Bilaal suggest kids can do to make a difference? Give examples. _____ _____ _____ _____ _____ _____ 2. What did Bilaal do to make a difference? _____ _____ _____ _____ _____ _____

Goals and Achievements

Student App Tracking Log

Place a check mark ✔ inside each circle on the chart below every time you complete or Fast Track a topic.

1	2	3	4	5	6	7	8	9	10	11	12	13
1.1	2.1	3.1	4.1	5.1	6.1	7.1	8.1	9.1	10.1	11.1	12.1	13.1
1.2	2.2	3.2	4.2	5.2	6.2	HFW	8.2	9.2	10.2	11.2	HFW	13.2
1.3	HFW	HFW	HFW	HFW	HFW	7.2	HFW	HFW	HFW	HFW	12.2	HFW
1.4	2.3	3.3	4.3	5.3	6.3	7.3	8.3	9.3	10.3	11.3	12.3	13.3
HFW	2.4	3.4	4.4	5.4	6.4	7.4	8.4	9.4	10.4	11.4	12.4	13.4
1.5	2.5	3.5	SP	SP	SP	7.5	8.5	SP	10.5	11.5	SP	SP
1.6	2.6	3.6				SP	8.6		10.6	SP		
SP	SP	SP					SP		SP			

HFW = High Frequency Words
SP = Success Passage

14	15	16	17	18	19	20	21	22	23	24	25
14.1	15.1	16.1	17.1	18.1	19.1	20.1	21.1	22.1	23.1	24.1	25.1
14.2	HFW	HFW	HFW	HFW	19.2	20.2	HFW	HFW	23.2	24.2	25.2
HFW	15.2	16.2	17.2	18.2	HFW	HFW	21.2	22.2	23.3	24.3	25.3
14.3	15.3	16.3	17.3	18.3	19.3	20.3	21.3	22.3	23.4	24.4	25.4
14.4	SP	SP	17.4	SP	19.4	20.4	21.4	SP	SP	24.5	SP
14.5			17.5		19.5	20.5	SP			SP	
SP			SP		SP	SP					

Success Reads Log

Each time you read a Success passage, write down the number of seconds it takes. Build your fluency.

Segment	Part 1 Seconds	Part 2 Seconds	Part 3 Seconds	Parts 1–3 Seconds
1. *Can You Nap?* Total Word Count: 118				
2. *Look! Nat Can Do That!* Total Word Count: 217				
3. *This Kid Did It!* Total Word Count: 178				
4. *Lin and Rex* Total Word Count: 121				
5. *A Big Yes to Less Plastic* Total Word Count: 282				
6. *Just Call Moz* Total Word Count: 198				
7. *Big Art* Total Word Count: 222				
8. *A Gift for Zak* Total Word Count: 309				
9. *A Big Trend* Total Word Count: 249				
10. *Catch That Trash!* Total Word Count: 201				
11. *From Page to Stage* Word Count: 286				
12. *What Is THAT Up There?* Total Word Count: 379				
13. *Humpback Hits* Total Word Count: 222				

Segment	Part 1 Seconds	Part 2 Seconds	Part 3 Seconds	Parts 1–3 Seconds
14. *Notes From the Amazon* Total Word Count: 246				
15. *Pains and Gains* Total Word Count: 290				
16. *Animals on the Move* Total Word Count: 296				
17. *I Didn't Say That!* Total Word Count: 349				
18. *Time to Act* Total Word Count: 211				
19. *Sports Stars* Total Word Count: 282				
20. *The Domino Contest* Total Word Count: 387				
21. *Tom Bass* Total Word Count: 288				
22. *A Timeless Treat* Total Word Count: 321				
23. *Use Your Noodles!* Total Word Count: 474				
24. *Lilly Ledbetter* Total Word Count: 299				
25. *The Goats of Mt. Etna* Total Word Count: 295				

Success Response Log

Keep track of the Success Series you have completed. Write the date that you finished the series. Then complete the sentence starter for each Success topic.

| Segment 1 | *Can You Nap?* |

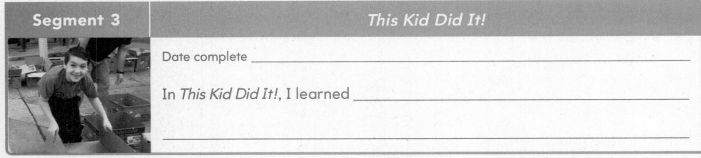

Date complete _____

In *Can You Nap?*, I learned _____

_____

| Segment 2 | *Look! Nat Can Do That!* |

Date complete _____

Look! Nat Can Do That! tells the story of _____

_____

| Segment 3 | *This Kid Did It!* |

Date complete _____

In *This Kid Did It!*, I learned _____

_____

| Segment 4 | *Lin and Rex* |

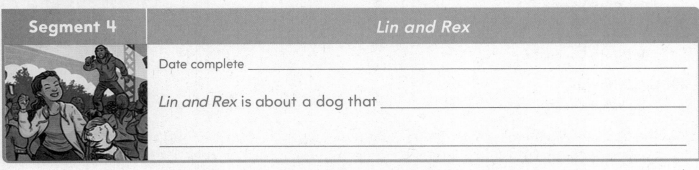

Date complete _____

Lin and Rex is about a dog that _____

_____

| Segment 5 | A Big Yes to Less Plastic |

Date complete _____

In *A Big Yes to Less Plastic*, _____

_____

| Segment 6 | Just Call Moz |

Date complete _____

Just Call Moz is about _____

_____

| Segment 7 | Big Art |

Date complete _____

In *Big Art*, artists create _____

_____

| Segment 8 | A Gift for Zak |

Date complete _____

A Gift for Zak tells the story of _____

_____

Success Response Log

Keep track of the Success Series you have completed. Write the date that you finished the series. Then complete the sentence starter for each Success topic.

Segment 9	*A Big Trend*

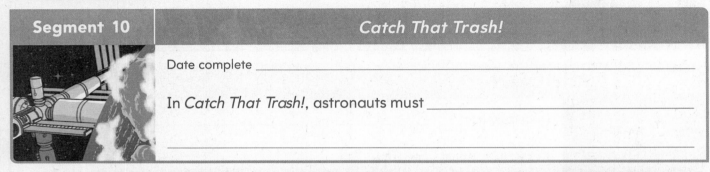

Date complete _____

In *A Big Trend*, I learned _____

_____

Segment 10	*Catch That Trash!*

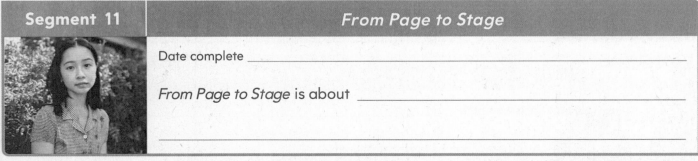

Date complete _____

In *Catch That Trash!*, astronauts must _____

_____

Segment 11	*From Page to Stage*

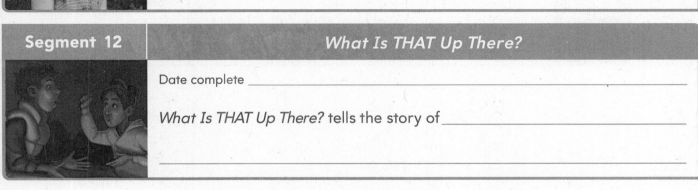

Date complete _____

From Page to Stage is about _____

_____

Segment 12	*What Is THAT Up There?*

Date complete _____

What Is THAT Up There? tells the story of _____

_____

Segment 13	Humpback Hits

Date complete _____

In *Humpback Hits*, I learned _____

_____

Segment 14	Notes From the Amazon

Date complete _____

The scientists in *Notes From the Amazon* _____

_____

Segment 15	Pains and Gains

Date complete _____

In *Pains and Gains*, I learned _____

_____

Segment 16	Animals on the Move

Date complete _____

Animals on the Move describes _____

_____

Success Response Log

Keep track of the Success Series you have completed. Write the date that you finished the series. Then complete the sentence starter for each Success topic.

Segment 17	*I Didn't Say That!*

Date complete _____

I Didn't Say That! is about _____

_____

Segment 18	*Time to Act*

Date complete _____

In *Time to Act*, I learned _____

_____

Segment 19	*Sports Stars*

Date complete _____

Sports Stars is about _____

_____

Segment 20	*The Domino Contest*

Date complete _____

The Domino Contest tells the story of _____

_____

Segment 21	Tom Bass

Date complete _____

In *Tom Bass*, I discovered _____

_____

Segment 22	A Timeless Treat

Date complete _____

A Timeless Treat is about _____

_____

Segment 23	Use Your Noodles!

Date complete _____

In *Use Your Noodles!*, contestants must _____

_____

Segment 24	Lilly Ledbetter

Date complete _____

In *Lilly Ledbetter*, I discovered _____

_____

Segment 25	The Goats of Mt. Etna

Date complete _____

The Goats of Mt. Etna tells about _____

_____

Acknowledgments

Excerpt from *Friends: True Stories of Extraordinary Animal Friendships* by Catherine Thimmesh. Text copyright © 2011 by Catherine Thimmesh. All rights reserved. Used by permission of HarperCollins Publishers.

Excerpt from *Making Change: Tips from an Underage Overachiever* by Bilaal Rajan. Text copyright © 2008 by Bilaal Rajan. All rights reserved. Used by permission of Orca Book Publishers.

Credits